# KNOWING WHERE WE ARE GOING

# Knowing Where We Are Going

## Contemporary Problems and the Christian Faith

A. N. TSIRINTANES

Translated by George A. Perris

CASSELL
LONDON

CASSELL & COMPANY LIMITED
35 Red Lion Square, London WC1R 4SG
and at Sydney, Auckland, Toronto, Johannesburg,
an affiliate of
Macmillan Publishing Co., Inc.,
New York

First published 1977

ISBN 0 304 29877 8

Printed in Great Britain by
The Camelot Press Ltd, Southampton

# Contents

|            |                                     | page |
|------------|-------------------------------------|------|
| Part One   | THE THEORY ABOUT ALL                |      |
|            | 1. The Fence                        | 3    |
|            | 2. Above the Fence                  | 13   |
|            | 3. Can Faith be Justified?          | 22   |
|            | 4. Moral Obligation                 | 33   |
| Part Two   | CHRISTIANITY                        |      |
|            | 5. Facing Christianity              | 45   |
|            | 6. The Natural Way                  | 60   |
|            | 7. Thus the Opportunity was Missed  | 68   |
|            | 8. When Atheism is a Leader         | 78   |
| Part Three | TOMORROW                            |      |
|            | 9. Tomorrow                         | 91   |
|            | 10. Being Up-to-date                | 99   |
|            | 11. The Fruits                      | 109  |

PART ONE

# The Theory about All

# I

# The Fence

i

It would be futile to try to stifle in ourselves the feeling of anxiety that besets mankind today or to escape by totally ignoring it. We can, however, and must (it is our sacred duty) do something far better. We can turn this feeling of anxiety into creative power.

To do this we must tell the truth. The whole truth. We must affirm that we are not only anxious for the future, but also disappointed in the past and conscious of the chaos of the present created by the fact that man has lost his way.

The man of today is like a ship that has lost her bearings on a stormy night because she has no compass, or rather because she has a demagnetized compass. Just like a ship, man needs a compass if he is not to lose his bearings but sail on a steady course. In other words he needs orientation.

This orientation is given by a general outlook on the world and life, by a theory about all that exists (a *Weltanschauung*) in the light of eternity. Without such a theory man will drift along without being conscious of where he is going.

With a theory like this as a guide man will explain and understand particular events and react according to the orientation given him by this theory. He will retain his own personality under any circumstances, even in the face of death. 'You can kill us,' he will say, like the Stoics or the early Christians, 'but you cannot harm us.' It is high time these words were heard again in our days.


ii


This theory, however, must fulfil certain conditions.

First of all it must be a world view that can stand the light of knowledge acquired by modern man, a world view that modern man could seriously, frankly, sincerely and honestly accept and take all the consequences.

Second, it must be accepted without *coercion*: not from the fear of the tyrant or of the police or of the judge: not from fear lest one should become a social outcast or be scorned by the masses; not even from the fear of God. So the believer should not believe in God because he fears Him but he should fear God because he believes in Him.

Third, this theory should serve as a *guide*, as a compass, so that man may lay down his course and follow it on his march to progress and elevation.

Fourth, it should provide man with support and not call on man to support it. It should then provide him with the peace of the Gospel, the comfortable feeling of the Stoics, the power to follow the course he intends to follow knowing where he is going. This would be the answer to the feeling of anxiety which possesses the soul of modern man.


iii


Such a theory should be man's—each man's—own world view. This, however, does not mean that it should be original or different from the world view of others. There is no doubt that to build up one's own world view one would benefit much by what others have said or written. Or one's world view may be simply an acceptance of what others have taught. But this should be done of one's own free will, without any coercion. In this case, one accepts the world view of somebody else and makes it one's own in full consciousness of what one is doing. Here, the reader may ask: 'Who am I to deal with such things? Is my stature high enough to do so?'

The answer is that there is simply no mortal man of such stature. If you say that any man or woman, even the wisest of all exponents of western civilization, is better fit to deal with a world theory than is the native of a savage country, you might as well say that a man at the top of the Alps is nearer to Sirius than is a mollusc at the bottom of the Pacific. This, however, does not mean that one should give up and let oneself drift with the tide instead of knowing where one is going. Quoting Hesiod's words, Socrates said: 'One must do what one can do.' And what one can do is to make a sincere and conscientious effort to lay down the course to be followed in one's life. This effort is every man's sacred duty.

These are the thoughts that induced the writer of this book to embark upon an endeavour to formulate a world view in the light of his conscience, and of a straightforward confrontation with reality. So he will try to expound, in all simplicity, his ideas about these great problems. Is he sure he will not be making mistakes? Not at all. But he can promise he will not say anything conventional, anything that he does not believe. He can promise to speak with sincerity and in good faith. This, in fact, is the only promise he can give the reader.

Here, then, follows the outcome of the writer's endeavour.

iv

I shall begin with a purely imaginary case somewhat reminiscent of the story of the Man in the Iron Mask.

5

Suppose a man was born and has grown in a room which he has not left, not even once in his life. He lives in complete isolation. He has never had any contact with the outside world which he has never seen or heard. In his room, which not even a ray of light can penetrate, darkness is dispelled only by an electric light.

Obviously, to this man his room is the whole world. Whatever he sees, hears or feels is in that room. The room is the only reality that this imaginary man can perceive. It is, as it were, his universe. But, objectively, it is not all. Outside there is an immense world of reality of which our man is not conscious. He does not even suspect its existence.

So for our man there are two realities. The one of which he is conscious. It is his room, his universe. The other is the immense reality which exists although its existence he does not even suspect.

Now suppose one day someone enters the room and takes our man to see another room in the same house. The next day he is taken to see the whole house and then he is led out to the street which he, of course, sees for the first time in his life. In this way our man's universe is constantly growing. It is not only his room any longer.

Actually, however, there has been no change in the fact that there are two realities. There is always the reality which our man perceives through his senses and the other reality, the immense reality, which he cannot perceive. That this man's universe was first a room and now a house with the part of the street outside it, makes no difference.

Yet, there *is* some difference. The expansion of the boundaries of the little universe our man had known shows that he was wrong when he thought (if he did) that there was nothing beyond the walls of his room. Now there is another room, or rooms and the street. The man begins to feel there is some other reality he cannot see yet. What that reality is he does not know, but he has no doubt there is something more beyond what he has seen until now, the existence of which he could not suspect when he was shut up in his room. Gradually he comes to this conclusion: The walls of his room were a kind of fence which permitted him to 'see' only an infinitesimal part of the reality that exists. Now this fence has receded, but has not been removed. Our man can see more now, but he has a stronger feeling of not having seen everything. He feels that there is a fence limiting the reality he has known until now and that beyond that fence there is more of that reality which he cannot perceive, but which nevertheless exists. His awareness of the fence becomes stronger each time the fence recedes, each time our man sees more of that reality whose existence he could not even suspect before.

Yet, besides the feeling of being confined inside a fence which prevents him from seeing the whole reality, our man has a desire to see more. And the more the fence recedes, letting him see new things, the stronger becomes his desire to know what there is on the other side of the fence.

Now suppose again that the liberator who led our man out of his prison, takes him, as Virgil took Dante, and shows him round the town or towns over the country; suppose he is allowed to set his eyes for the first time on a starry sky at night. What difference does this make? None at all. Our man is still under the impression of a finite world which he can perceive and has the same desire to get a glimpse of the reality that exists beyond the fence.

And suppose our man is taken by his Virgil or, if you prefer, his Beatrice to Mount Palomar—or, if you like, a super Mount Palomar—Observatory and there he looks at the stars and the galaxies and the whole astronomical Universe. 'Well now,' he may say, 'I have seen everything. The fence has been removed. What I see now is all the reality that exists.' His Virgil, however, affably dispels his illusion. He takes him to see a drop of water under a powerful microscope and lo and behold the fence is there again.

v

Has the microscope brought us to the end? Surely not. There is the world of anti-matter and the immense problems and questions that it raises. There is also the world of the spirit or if you like man's inner world and its vicissitudes. Besides the universe of the astronomer there is the world of hatred, of love, and heroism. How can one explore this world?

But that is not all. There are so many 'whys' and 'hows' to be answered. There is the problem of 'causes' (and thence that of the prime cause and of the question 'where do we come from?'), and the problem of the 'essence and the meaning of life'. Our man now sees that the fence is always receding but never pulled down. But he wants it removed. He turns to his guide and says: 'When shall I be able to see, understand and perceive *everything*, all the reality that exists?'

Here our modern Virgil would answer perhaps with the statement of one of the later English philosophers, C. E. M. Joad, who said that he could not understand why the universe should be so made as to be contained in the mind of a man of the twentieth century, or with the statement of Einstein that he could not see why the universe should be such as to be understood by man. Or he would try to put the whole thing in a nutshell by suggesting something simple, something that I will attempt to present in the form of a mathematical formula. This formula consists of only two symbols: *a*

8

and $\infty$: $a$ stands for what man perceives either through his senses or through his 'reason': it is the reality we can feel, perceive, verify or control. While $\infty$ stands for the whole reality, everything that exists. Our formula then would be: $a < \infty$. Whatever the value of $a$, it is always less than infinity. In other words, the value of $a$, its extent in the world that is perceivable by man, may continuously increase with the progress of science, human thought or technology, but it will always be less than infinity.

To the farmer of Hesiod's time the value of $a$ was, say, 1: to Aristotle, perhaps, 1,000: to the man of today —the man of the space age—say, 1,000,000 or perhaps 100,000,000: to the man 500 years hence, the value of $a$ may reach 1,000,000,000. But whatever that value may be, it will never reach infinity. The fence that sets the bounds of human knowledge may recede from the four walls of a room to the galaxies, but it will always be a fence. There will always be reality beyond its bounds, reality that transcends man's universe and is not liable to human control. It is, if I may use the term, 'supra-controllable' reality.

This 'supra-controllable' reality is of two kinds. First there is the reality which, to the man of today, is outside the fence but to the man of tomorrow may well be inside it. The power of steam and electricity was beyond the fence to our forefathers and so was atomic power to prewar man. And who knows what reality will be revealed to the man of tomorrow which the man of today cannot even suspect?

But there is also another kind of reality. Our distance from that reality is the same now as it was in the time of Hesiod and there is no reason to suggest that it will not be the same after thousands of years.

It is the reality of metaphysics. Let me explain. I can imagine man reaching the outer planets and even fixed

9

stars some day. But I cannot imagine *how* man can, by any observation, experiment or calculation, ever get knowledge of such matters as how the world was created or not created; how life came to the world (even experiments of artificial generation of life cannot prove how life *actually* came to this planet); whether there is life after death and in what form.

Before these matters can be checked, it is the receiving capacity of the human mind and not man's knowledge that should be enlarged. For here the fence consists in the limitation of our receiving capacity and not in the insufficiency of images received. As long as there is no change in these conditions—or as long as the human brain does not change, as materialists would put it—the human mind—or, if you like, the human brain—will never be able to deal with these things either at present or in future. Here one cannot help recalling Dubois-Reymond's words 'ignoramus et ignorabimus'.

In short, what we have called 'supra-controllable' reality may be divided into two parts: (a) the reality *beyond* the fence (which is on the same level as that of the inside of the fence); and (b) the reality *above* the fence. As the fence recedes, it takes in continuously some of the reality which was previously beyond it, but it will never take in any of the reality *above* it, for that reality lies always outside the receiving capacity of the human mind. The reality of the second type we call 'supernatural'. Thus, by the term 'supernatural' we mean not what is simply beyond the fence, *viz* beyond our present knowledge, but what is above the fence, *viz* what cannot be conceived by the faculties of the human mind. Now, if someone tells me there is no reality that cannot be conceived by the human mind, I can only say I do not see how such an argument can be supported.

Moreover, the fact that I cannot see (or generally perceive) everything that exists does not mean that what

I cannot see does not exist. If you say that this sort of reasoning is commonplace so much the better. But, unfortunately, it is not. The sage who, having observed the universe through a telescope, said that he had not seen God anywhere on the lenses of that telescope and that, therefore, God did not exist, was talking pure nonsense. His argument was based on a false proposition, namely, that everything that exists can be seen. This is the fundamental lie that has given rise to many an absurd and ruinous theory.

The fence may recede, but it can never be pulled down. It is always there, embarrassing us. The imaginary man of our story would feel the same embarrassment before this fence as he had felt when he was confined within the four walls of his room; and he would have the same desire to see what lies on the other side of the fence, even if it were large enough to embrace the extreme boundaries of the universe as they are revealed by the telescope of the Mount Palomar Observatory.

So, every man or woman is conscious of this fence and longs to see what there is beyond it. And the more it recedes the stronger becomes our desire to climb over it.

vi

What I have said about the fence should not lead the reader to believe that it is a long way off, and that it ends somewhere in the outer space which we can observe through our telescope. We can see it in every function of our day-to-day life; even in the simplest functions of our reason when, for instance, we want to explain the causes of the various phenomena and reach up to the *prime cause*. We can see it when we try to comprehend the phenomenon of *life*. Life is, of course, described by

B

Philosophy and Science, but in a way that makes our formula $a < \infty$ still more evident.

The more we investigate, the more perceptible the fence becomes. It separates the conceivable from the inconceivable, the controllable from the uncontrollable. It goes through man's inner world and divides it into two parts. I would say that man is the meeting place of the two realities, the 'controllable' and the 'supra-controllable' or in other words the natural and the supernatural.

The encounter of these two realities in man generates what we call human personality.

Let me refer to one expression of this encounter. Often the two realities meet in the instinct of self-preservation. That instinct is something natural, perceivable, located inside the fence. To overcome the instinct of self-preservation, to sacrifice one's life willingly for the sake of a value one believes (rightly or wrongly) to be higher than one's life is a reality, exceptional perhaps, but not too rare in history both past and present. To explain this reality one must climb over the fence to the realm of the supernatural. We can, therefore, conclude that, as I said before, the human personality is the meeting place of the two worlds: the natural and the supernatural.

# 2

# Above the Fence

What I have stated about the 'fence' that sets a limit
to human knowledge and about the realities beyond the
limits of human knowledge or human control (beyond
the fence) and especially the realities above those limits
(above the fence) brings us face to face with the philosophical trend which, since Thomas Huxley, has been
known as 'agnosticism' (a Greek word denoting the
doctrine that nothing is known or likely to be known
beyond material phenomena).

In its extreme form, agnosticism leads to the concept
that man knows nothing about anything. Here, however,
I mean agnosticism as the idea that the ultimate origin of
the universe and of all beings is completely unknown
to man and that there cannot be any metaphysical
science.

From what I have said it is obvious that according to
the idea which serves as a basis to this investigation, all
metaphysical questions are, as it were, 'above the fence'.
To these questions we have no answer today and, as I
said before, we are not likely to have one tomorrow or in
the future.

So, if 'agnosticism' meant nothing but to admit that
we have no answer to metaphysical questions and that
there can be no science of metaphysics; if it meant
nothing but to confess, like Dubois-Reymond, that 'we
are ignorant and we shall always be so' (*ignoramus et*

*ignorabimus*) we would have no objection to agreeing with it.

Since Huxley, however, agnosticism has moved further on. It is no longer consistent with its basic principle and although it denounces metaphysics as a science, it puts up its own metaphysical theories to which it attributes the name and prestige of science.

The question in this case is the point at which one enters the region of metaphysics. The agnostic seems to think that one enters that region when one *gives* a certain *answer*, when in fact one does so when one *puts* a certain *question*. If, for instance, you ask about the origin of the world you are already in the region of metaphysics whether you answer that 'the world was made by God' or that 'the world has some other origin and that, therefore, there is no God'. In both cases you are 'above the fence' and you do 'not know'.

Man therefore enters the region of metaphysics as soon as he attempts to cross the border and rise above the 'fence' of his knowing capacity. This is where 'knowledge' ends and 'faith' begins. And this is true of any metaphysical concept. The answer to a question belonging to the metaphysical sphere will necessarily be a proposition of faith and not a datum of knowledge. He who declares his belief in one God is as much a believer as was Spinoza when he asserted his formula *Deus sive natura*, as is the materialist or anyone who upholds Monod's ideas. They all have their *credos* without suspecting it just like Molière's Monsieur Jourdain who for more than forty years had been speaking prose without knowing it.

The conflict here is between the various *credos* and not between faith and science as is contended by many. Such a contention (you answer fundamental questions through faith and I answer them through science) is simply a lie. No science working with scientific methods has ever set forth a proposition entering the region of metaphysics.

Now, a few words about the believer, especially the Christian believer who would perhaps be offended if told that he had no knowledge of metaphysical questions. 'I have no knowledge,' he would say, 'but I have faith. To me faith is tantamount or perhaps superior to knowledge. Through faith I can see God. If you do not share in my faith, I am sorry for you, but this will not prevent me from seeing things through faith.' Yet St Paul says: 'Faith is the evidence of things not seen.' To the believer faith ranks higher than knowledge, but in fact it is not knowledge. The Creator has not made us omniscient. He has made us mortal with limited powers of thinking and knowing. Beyond the boundaries of knowledge there is faith, whether it is our faith or the faith of those who oppose it.

ii

To explain my attitude towards *positivism* I should say that to me it is a matter of consistency and sincerity in view also of the boundaries within which positivism claims to be valid. In other words if positivism accepts only positive facts and observable phenomena, especially the realities that can be put to the test by physical science, what about the realities which cannot be so tested? Positivism has every right to say that it does not know about things that cannot be put to the test of science. But it has no right to say that it knows (how does it?) there is no reality beyond that which can be checked by science, for no scientific test has ever proved the truth of this argument. It is an argument supported only by the fallacy of human omniscience according to which man knows 'positively' everything and whatever is not known or knowable by man, simply does not exist.

If positivism said that beyond the 'positive' there was no *human knowledge*, it would be a theory consistent with itself. But when it says that beyond the 'positive' there is no reality it becomes an irresponsible and inconsistent theory. In this case positivism identifies the boundaries of knowledge with the infiniteness of reality which is absurd and contrary to experience on which positivism purports to be based. For everyday experience reveals new realities which were not 'positively' known before and therefore—according to positivism's way of thinking —non-existent!

One would have no objection to the assertion of positivism, *viz* that metaphysics lies outside the field of 'positive' knowledge. But when positivism creates its own kind of metaphysics (or even pseudo-metaphysics), when it enters the metaphysical sphere by putting up its propositions about metaphysical questions, even if such propositions are negative (there is no God), then it simply proves itself contradictory. For this reason, positivism cannot be atheistic without being contradictory, and, as I said before, not only faith in God but also any concept about the first cause of being falls within the region of metaphysics. The same holds true in respect of other metaphysical questions whether viewed in the light of faith—especially Christian faith— or of any other concept or even of 'pure negation'.

### iii

Our stand towards the problem of evidence in metaphysical matters has been made clear by what I have said in the foregoing paragraphs.

Two persons, A and B, have different views on the metaphysical question. A accepts the existence of God,

B accepts something else as the prime cause of being or that there is no such cause at all. With which of these two persons rests the onus of proof?

The general rule will have to be applied. Each of them will have to give evidence of the truth of his argument. A will be asked to prove the existence of God, B the other reality which he thinks to have been the cause of beings.

Yet, things are not so simple. For A, the believer, will say (if he wants to speak frankly) that he can prove nothing. (The so-called proofs of the existence of God have now been generally abandoned.) But he will add that his inability to give evidence of the truth of his argument is due to the human mind, as I have said before. No one can prove anything about these matters. Therefore, A asserts his faith instead of giving evidence. B, on the other hand, has to choose between two alternatives. The one is to deny A's statement that of necessity we take recourse to faith, that is, to assert that such matters *can* be proved—in which case he must give *real proof* in support of his assertion. For B cannot prove his own assertion merely by saying that A has not proved his. The alternative is for B to admit that no proof can be given in respect of such matters and assert anything he likes not as a proof but as a *credo*.

The matter needs further explanation: B cannot say to A: 'You have not proved your assertion, therefore *my* assertion is true.' For B cannot rest on a mere denial, but must make his own concrete assertion and prove it. Otherwise, A might just as well say: 'You have not proved your assertion, therefore *my* assertion is true.'

All these, however, could be said for the sake of argument. To get to the heart of the matter we should admit that of metaphysical matters no proof or evidence whatsoever can be given. This, of course, does not mean that he who believes does so blindly and without reason. He certainly has his reason or reasons that justify his faith. With this justification we shall deal later on.

Just a few words—I needn't say more—about indifference to metaphysical matters. Those who are indifferent to the question of God's existence are truly atheists. For to think that one can be indifferent about God is tantamount to renouncing God.

iv

In the preceding chapters we dealt, in some detail, with the barrier (the 'fence' as I called it) that confines our knowledge of reality within certain, albeit always expanding, bounds. We gave the formula $a < \infty$ to represent the relation between knowable and non-knowable reality. We referred particularly to the 'fence' that limits our knowledge, the fence which is constantly receding but never removed. We also referred to the reality 'about the fence'. About that reality modern man knows nothing more than primitive man. On the other hand, man's desire to soar above the 'fence' and see what it hides, is also a reality. Always and everywhere man has had the desire to know what there is beyond the things he can see, and how the things he can see were called into existence; whether there is a prime cause, a Power that has made the world and, if so, how our relations with that Power can be determined; how we can please or displease It; whether we can communicate with It; whether there is, for us, life beyond the grave. With all these metaphysical questions men of all races and of all times, have, consciously or unconsciously, dealt. Much has, of course, been said about these questions by men of various nations, races, traditions and religions, under various geographical, economic or social conditions. Much that is not only dissimilar but also conflicting. Hosts of scholars were in the past and are now occupied with, and enormous libraries have been set up for the study of, these conflicting views. Yet, there are some points which coincide—points on which men of various races and ages agree, as if by biological necessity.

In the course of centuries or rather millennia, men belonging to races that had never seen one another— Lapps or Congolese; Europeans or natives of South America; ancient Greeks or barbarians mentioned by Herodotus—entertained certain beliefs known and accepted by all men in such a way as to become common to all mankind across the barriers of space and time.

v

They can be summed up into four propositions.

The **first proposition** is the existence of a *Power* which surpasses the power of men and which has created the world. At this moment we will not consider the fact that men think of this Power in a different way, some as one god, some as many gods, some as a spirit, some as a carved image, some as a good, providing father, some as an evil power. The fact is that they all see a *Creating Power* and no matter how coarse the husk is that surrounds the kernel, they all agree, as far as their mental development permits, to the existence of a supernatural Creator of the universe, of a Prime Cause.

Our first proposition then is the existence of a *superhuman, supernatural Creating Power*.

The **second proposition** is the belief entertained by most people, that this *Creating Power* did not just create the world and then leave it to its fate, but it is still in contact with the world and takes care of it as a *Governor and Provider*. There are, of course, numerous ways in which the various peoples of the earth imagine this Providence to work. Some think of It as an affectionate father, some as a revenging or even ill-doing power, but the fact is that all people—whether developed or primitive—accept in their own way (be it refined or rough) that the Creating Power is in perpetual contact with its creatures and provides for them. So the second proposition is about what we may call *Divine Providence*.

The **third proposition** is this: From the depths of the ages to this day, at least before atheistic propaganda could bear fruit, man has never been on good terms with the idea that death will put an end to his existence. He finds it hard to believe that his personal being disappears with the destruction of his body. He somehow believes in some sort of survival after death, in a life 'beyond the grave'. Either by teaching or by custom; either through the door or through the window, the idea that man lives somehow after death, penetrates the human mind.

This idea of *survival* or *immortality* takes various forms depending on man's particular cultural environment. Some people may believe in immortality through survival in a world of spirits, or in a new material world; some savage tribes may believe that man survives in the body of his children if he is eaten by them; other people believe in metempsychosis; in any case they all accept the proposition of a life beyond the grave.

Along with the second proposition about Providence or God's care for us, the belief in a life beyond the grave is also connected with the idea of some kind of recompense given man in the other life, a *reward* for the good or *punishment* for the evil he did in this life.

Among culturally more developed peoples there is also the idea of man's supra-material existence in the form of an *immortal soul*.

The **fourth proposition** refers to man's contact with his Creator. This contact may be made before the altar or through prayer, any prayer in noble or even empty words. Or, as in the early periods of history, through the sacrifice of animals or even human sacrifice. In any case the altar is a universal phenomenon. As Plutarch says, you may see cities without the amenities of civilized life, but not without sanctuaries.*

In our days, of course, man has tried to build cities without sanctuaries. But this is a purely artificial experiment. It cannot abolish an age-long tradition. In any case whether cities without sanctuaries and men who do not pray can look forward to a prosperous future, has yet to be proved.

* In your travels you may come upon cities without walls, writing, king, houses or property, doing without currency, having no notion of a theatre or gymnasium; but a city without holy places and gods, without any observance of prayers, oaths, oracles, sacrifices for blessings received or rites to avert evils, no traveller has ever seen or will ever see. No, I think a city might rather be formed without the ground it stands on than a government, once you remove all religion from under it, get itself established or once established survive. Plutarch, *Reply to Colotes*, 1125 e. Translated by B. Einarson and Ph. de Lacy: Loeb Classical Library.

# 3

# Can Faith be Justified?

The four propositions we have just examined refer to realities 'above the fence' which we cannot verify either at present or in the future through observation, even if we use radio telescopes and electronic computers perfected to the highest degree. Nor can we ever expect to conceive these realities unless our human mind is so changed as to acquire special knowing capacities.

So, the content of these propositions cannot be proved. They are simply propositions of faith. Lack of proof, however, is no reason why a proposition should be rejected unless it is *susceptible of proof*. But in this case, the subject of these propositions is such as not to allow for any possibility of being checked by the human mind, and the more so when it deals with realities 'above the fence'. In this case neither the content of the proposition can be proved, nor is the lack of such proof any evidence of the falsity of the proposition, and much less of the truth of the opposite one.

Above all, although these propositions cannot be proved they are not irresponsible. They are not at all without *support* or, a reasonable basis on which they can stand. A proposition is admissible when, although it cannot be proved, it can, however, be accepted as true and be trusted for a very good reason.

## ii

Let me quote an example from everyday life. If I get seriously ill, I call a doctor and I put my life in his hands. He gives me all sorts of drugs or pills to take while I cannot prove at all whether they will make me well or they will send me to the next world too early. Or I may let him take me to the operating table and cut up or sew up my insides. I have no idea of what he is doing and I can prove nothing about the correctness of his actions. Yet, I take it for granted that I must trust him. And for a very good reason. You see the man is a doctor. So I am right in trusting him and I would be wrong if I did not. In my eyes the man is 'legalized' to act the way he does because he is an MD and his capacity as such is supported by his experience, his reputation and other qualities. In this case I am ignorant, but the doctor knows. But in metaphysical questions not only I, but the whole of mankind is ignorant. Yet the analogy exists. These propositions cannot be proved but they can be legalized, in the sense that man has a very good reason to accept them as true and let them direct his life.

## iii

The justifying grounds for accepting these four propositions are subject to the following conditions:

First, that they refer to matters which are not susceptible of proof. They cannot be proved because they lie beyond the capacity of the human brain to verify or refute them;

Second, that the content of these propositions *is not opposed* to things which, being susceptible to the scrutiny of the human mind, have already been *checked and proved*. A proposition like this must not be contrary to what the human mind can check and prove right; and

Third, that they can be *reasonably deduced*. I must accept these propositions upon good grounds. To me these propositions are of validity because I have good grounds for accepting them in the same way as the doctor's opinion is of validity because I have good grounds (his medical degree) for accepting it. Needless to say—but perhaps I should say it—the grounds on which my deduction is supported must not be an object of faith but a tangible fact which should lie inside the 'fence' so that I can check it and prove it true. In other words what I use in support of the reasonableness of my faith should not be accepted 'by faith' but as 'a fact' that can be checked. From what I can check then I can deduce what I cannot check. The reader may remark that I have said nothing about intuition as expounded mainly by Bergson. I do not object to this theory but I do not need it in the present study.

1. This holds good in respect of *science*. What man can check—not conjecture!—through science, under appropriate scientific procedure, cannot be revoked by such propositions. That the earth is a sphere cannot be disproved by passages from the Bible as it had been attempted in the past.

2. What was said about science is also true of logic. I cannot admit things that my reason has rejected. I do not say, though, I cannot admit things that my reason cannot conceive because they surpass the knowing capacity of my mind. *Such kind of 'rationalism' would not be at all rational*, for, as we saw before, nothing can lead us to the conclusion that the universe is so made as to be

comprehended by the human brain. But I cannot accept things which can be conceived by the human mind, things which lie within the 'fence', if my reason has rejected them as irrational. I may put it this way. I accept what is *above reason*, but not what is *against reason*. I can accept what my reason *cannot* conceive, but I cannot accept what my reason *can* conceive and rejects as irrational or contradictory. And if you say: 'How do you know your reason works well?' I will answer: 'This is the reason I use as a guide in my life. If you try to persuade me to change it I can understand you. But I cannot construct a reason ad hoc to fit in with yours by accepting your proposition, even if it appears as a proposition of faith.'

3. Moreover, these propositions should not be contrary to moral command as my conscience accepts it.\* I cannot allow things which I reject as immoral to be vested with the authority of supernatural truth. And if you ask me again how do I know my conscience is not wrong I will say: 'This is the conscience I have. If you think it works wrong, prove it. But don't ask me to construct a conscience ad hoc to fit in with your propositions.'

iv

Now, on the basis of the foregoing I shall deal with the legitimization of the above propositions in particular.

The first condition (that the propositions refer to matters not susceptible of proof) is fulfilled, as there is no doubt that these propositions cannot be proved because they refer to matters not susceptible of proof. They refer

---

\* The doctrine of predestination—according to which there are people who will be condemned to eternal damnation since 'God has made them to be so'—will help my readers to understand what I mean.

to matters which lie 'above the fence' (supernatural) and, therefore, cannot be proved.

The second condition (that the content of these propositions is not opposed to things already checked and proved) is also fulfilled because these propositions are not contrary to things already checked and proved.

No one has ever really produced any scientific datum opposed to these propositions. Neither my reason nor my moral conscience find it difficult to accept them. On the contrary the statement 'every house has its founder; and the founder of all is God' (Heb. 3, 4), is an example of impeccable reasoning.

Now I come to the third condition, namely, that these propositions can be reasonably deduced. The fact that these four propositions have been accepted always, everywhere and by all (*semper ubique ab omnibus*), the fact that a general agreement on them has been an age-long tradition from the depths of unrecorded time, is good ground for their being reasonably deduced. This fact can be easily checked by man, because it lies 'within the fence'. I can examine and check it whenever I like. I can do this checking once, twice, many times. You may call me naïve. It is not always bad to be naïve. But I do not see why, under these circumstances, I should give up these propositions which the human race—beyond any bounds of colour, time, distance or climate—has accepted from time immemorial and adopt other propositions contrary to them which also I cannot prove, and that without having the decency to admit that they cannot be proved.

v

These four propositions vary, however, as to clarity. They are not equally clear to human perception. This is more evident in respect of the propositions about Providence and immortality of the soul.

In fact, faith in Divine Providence seems to be weakened by the question of how, if there is a god who provides for everything, there is so much natural or moral evil in the world. Just think of the accursed disease of cancer or the moral evil which has infested mankind for whole ages and that *in the name of God*. Here the subject of 'theodicy' appears to be an obstacle to faith. There are many books about theodicy but I will express my thoughts on this subject in a few lines.

Theodicy is put forward in two senses. First as a question: Why is there evil in the world, since God governs the world? This question is quite reasonable. After all one may ask the same thing about any government. So it is quite natural that it should be asked about the government of God. It should not be considered as an insult to the Creator if we really believe that He has created men to think as free beings and if we must take seriously the words of St Paul: 'You are no longer a slave but a son.' (Gal. 4, 7) As a son, man is quite justified in asking.

Well, what is the answer that the writer gives himself in reply to this very reasonable question? The answer is: 'I do not know. And I am not satisfied with any of the answers given from various quarters. Moreover, I am sorry to disappoint the reader, but I have no answer to give either. I simply do not know why there is so much evil in the world, since there is Divine Providence.'

Now what does this prove?

Here we come to the second sense in which theodicy is meant. It is the conclusion that since we do not know of any justifying reason why there are things which we call evil, there is *no such justifying reason* and therefore there is no Providence.

In this second sense theodicy is a sophism. It starts

c

with the following major premise: 'If there was a justifying reason for this thing, I should have known it: I do not know such a reason, therefore such a reason does not exist.' The argument leads further to the conclusion that since there are things for which no reason exists, there is no Providence.

All this is but a series of sophisms which can be refuted in the same way as before: 'that I do not see something is not a proof that it does not exist.'

The matter, however, presents another aspect, quite reverse to the previous one, which, by logical necessity, follows from the statement that there is no Providence or Provider. In other words, one may ask, 'If there is no Providence or Creator how can we explain the fact that there is so much order and "finality" in the world?' You see reason works both ways. There are also arguments supporting 'a-theodicy'. How can we explain the order that prevails and all the good that exists in the world, supposing there is no God? So, it is quite reasonable to adopt the following conclusion: in our contact with the world we often see Providence at work. In some cases, however, we do not. But this does not mean that we should forget the cases when we *do* see It.

Let me make myself clearer. I find it hard, sometimes very hard, to understand how Providence permits so much evil, above all moral evil, to be manifested in the world—and that in the name of the Almighty—I find it hard to answer to some (not all) of the objections put up by Lucian against Providence.* But I find it impossible to give a negative answer to Socrates on the questions he put to Aristodemus about the order which prevails in the world (Xenophon, *Memorabilia* I, 4 1 seq. and IV, 3 2 seq.), and that in the light of science at the close of the twentieth century. How many things

---

* In his 'Ζεύς Τραγωδός' (Jupiter the Tragedian).

thought to be 'aimless' in the past have now been proved to be very useful in the course of history and in the light of modern science!

Obviously, then, I cannot exclude the possibility that a good deal of modern man's doubts may be dispelled by the light of tomorrow in the same way that the light of today has dispelled many of the doubts of the past. For instance, progress in biological sciences has revealed the usefulness of some of the organs of the human body hitherto considered quite useless.

vi

We now come to the matter of man's survival after death, of a life 'beyond the grave', of immortality. Lack of clarity in this matter is made more pronounced by the fact that the doctrine of immortality is not clearly formulated in all religions. But even where there is no complete doctrine about this matter, there is at least a rudimentary idea about man's survival after death and in any case man's annihilation is nowhere an accepted doctrine. And as Christ once observed, when the Old Testament calls upon Abraham and Isaac and Jacob, it does not call upon annihilated but upon living beings (Matt. 22, 32). Even where there is no concrete doctrine about man's survival after death, or, respectively, the resurrection of the dead, the idea of immortality still exists in depth. Peoples who do not know about immortality are no strangers to the idea of some kind of survival after death. As far as the idea of immortality is concerned, these peoples are, as it were, underdeveloped.

So, there remains only one argument against the idea of immortality: that one fails to realize what life would be like after the decomposition of the human body. But as we have already seen this argument cannot stand. If, for instance, I cannot imagine what living beings would be like on another planet, this does not mean that such beings could not exist. To the followers of materialism the idea of immortality is not admissible. To them, the decomposition of the human body is tantamount to the annihilation of human personality, because they identify the body with the personality, or at least they regard the latter as a product of the former. But as I do not happen to be a materialist; as I do not think that I exist only as matter; as I do not fall in with the views of Feuerbach (expressed in his long-forgotten but recently resuscitated motto *Der Mensch ist was er isst*—man is what he eats), I cannot see on what grounds the argument against immortality can be supported. I cannot see why the decomposition of my body should necessarily bring about the annihilation of my personality; and why I should reject the proposition concerning immortality—which, as we saw, is perfectly admissible—just because I cannot imagine what life after death would be like.

vii

Yet, between faith and unbelief there is also the reality of doubt. This reality is more clearly manifested today.

In the life of modern man—including some of the noblest men or women of our times—doubt plays an important role. There are lots of people today who are neither staunch believers nor outright atheists. I do not know (I am not a searcher of men's hearts and thoughts) how many people believe so much as not to be disturbed by doubt. Yet, there are quite a few atheists who are not cocksure about their atheism and wonder whether something of what faith says may not, after all, be true.

To the man of today doubt is, then, a sort of psychological reality. A reality we can neither ignore nor condemn. Let us not be deceived. Doubt is an extremely trying experience. But it is not blameworthy, contemptible or morally wrong. It is lack of consistency in what we say we believe and not doubt about matters of faith that is morally wrong. We must, therefore, try to understand those who doubt. This understanding is part of our duty to truth, to our fellow-humans and to ourselves.

No one has the right to blame people—especially today's people—for doubting. And least of all the faithful Christian who should admit that, on the part of Christianity, much has been done for twenty centuries and is still being done to justify doubt in the hearts of people. Besides, our age is not at all encouraging to faith. Every day, new theories, alleged to have the support of science, are propounded which seem to strengthen unbelief. Atheism has almost universally been established and (*terribile dictu!*) the slogan 'God is dead' is adopted by theologians and bishops. All these things constitute, of course, a strong encouragement to doubt. And I do not know if there is any faithful Christian on earth who would be justified in casting a stone against a doubter as if to him, the faithful, doubt were an unknown experience.

Here, however, I should make it clear that what I have said about doubt refers to the sincere, honest and consistent kind of doubt. Not to the 'doubt' that serves as a disguise of negation and unbelief. Here I refer to the doubter who makes allowance for both sides of the question; who counts on the possibility that faith may be true and who is consistent with his doubts; who sets the course of his life in view of the possibility that faith both as a fact and as a moral obligation may be real. Whenever the faithful meets such doubt, honest, sincere and consistent doubt, let him not discard it. He may find a use for it. For all he knows it may be the preamble of faith. After all Jesus did not turn down but helped the man who said to Him, 'I have faith, help me where faith falls short.' (Mark 9, 24)

# 4

# Moral Obligation

i

We now come to a completely new world. From the world of 'what is' (ὄν: the world of reality) we come to the world of 'what ought to be' (δέον); or, in other words, to the world of moral obligation.

Human conscience is the centre and power in the deontological view of the world. The main task of conscience is to serve as a counterweight to instinct which dictates only what is expedient to us or to our ego. Conscience, on the other hand, dictates our moral obligation or duty, which may not be expedient to us and it may even ask for the sacrifice of our ego.

Before we go any further into the matter I should like to say this. It is somehow difficult to grasp why, even with people whose conscience is very sensitive, the content of moral obligation varies from one person to another. What person A feels to be his duty according to the dictates of his conscience, is sometimes quite different from what person B thinks to be right in the same way.

But this is mostly the result of a secondary process. The writer thinks that if all men, in all geographical longitudes and latitudes, were not influenced by various external trends or other factors, they would feel about the same as to their moral obligations. But even if my opinion is not right, the fact is that, in bold outline, duty is clear to all. Every man responds to the admonition 'always treat others as you would like them to treat you'.

Ulpian's precepts (*juris praecepta*)—'live honestly, do nobody any harm, give every man his own'—are heard throughout the world. Love is something everyone desires, even those who do not feel it for others. In essential matters, every man's conscience says the same thing. If there is doubt as to what is right, my conscience at least tells me that I should do what I think right and just even if it is against my own interests. This is the essence of my conscience's command which is the foundation of the world of moral obligation.

And now let us lay down the fundamental principle that governs moral obligation. In the world of reality we have laid down a primary, absolute, basic proposition. The whole reality will always be greater than the reality we can check. There will always be some reality we cannot check. The universe, we said before, is not all.

In the world of moral obligation we will set forth a similar basic proposition: 'Ego is not All.' As far as moral obligation is concerned, I am not all. I must not make myself the exclusive object of my pursuits and activities. I must go further into the realm of the 'super-self'.

ii

A man who cares only for himself is not a natural being. *Egocentrism is an abnormal condition.*

The being that lives for and is interested only in itself is not an efficient human being. We would even put up this definition: 'Man is the being that goes out of its "self" and moves up to its "super-self".'

In conclusion we would say this. As is known, science, philosophy and even common human thinking group men into various categories, races, nations, professional or social classes, political beliefs and the like. We would say that above all these groups and distinctions between men, the basic or fundamental distinction which we have not heeded—and we are punished for that—is the one referring to two types of men. On the one hand we have the man who is dominated entirely by his ego, who is interested only in himself. Even when he turns his eyes to Heaven he does it to serve his own interests and his own plans, lawful or even unlawful. He is the man to whom holiness is what Plato calls an 'art of barter'.* Even his relations with God are carried out on a commercial basis.

On the other hand, we have the man of 'super-self'. He is the man who sees himself as the servant of his fellow-humans; he is anxious about the future of the whole; he gets annoyed when others are wronged, although he himself has nothing to lose; he identifies his interests, his desires, his sorrows, his joys with those of his fellow-men. Even his own personal improvement he regards as a means to make himself more useful and more serviceable to the whole. To this type of man, the fulfilment of moral obligation is the supreme target. He rejoices at doing his duty. And even if he serves his own interests, this type of man does so under the impression, right or wrong, that by so doing he serves the interests of the whole.

Further, I should make it clear that the former of the two types of man should not be confused with another type of man to which it is very similar. There is also the man of unselfish ego who thinks, erroneously or stupidly perhaps, that he, only, is able 'to do the job properly' and that all the others should obey him without question. As is, for instance, the paterfamilias of the traditional

---

* Plato, *Euthyphro* 18.
    *Socrates:* Their holiness would be an art of barter between gods
      and men.
    *Euthyphro:* Yes, of barter if you like to call it so.
Translated by H. N. Fowler, The Loeb Classical Library.

type who wants all the members of his family to obey his orders because he thinks, rightly or wrongly, that, by so doing, he acts in the best interests of his family for whose sake he is ready to sacrifice his own. Such a man may perhaps be called an autocrat, but he is not an egoist. His attitude is not commendable, of course, but it has nothing to do with the attitude of the individualist to whom we have referred.

We have said that the man of 'super-self' may pursue what is profitable to him provided it serves also the interests of the whole. Yet there are people who ignore their own selves completely for the sake of others. If not completely eliminated, their 'self' is almost lost in the desire to serve aims which relate to the region of their 'super-self'. Such people are examples of the heroic type of man; the man who sacrifices himself to heroic aims, to aims belonging to the sphere of the 'super-self'. There are cases where the heroic action of this type of man may involve the sacrifice of his life. But it may also take the form of a life of complete disregard of 'self'. This kind of sacrifice is, perhaps, higher than the sacrifice of life in the literal sense, because it goes on for a long time and has not the splendour of the halo of a martyr.

In conclusion, I would say this. There are only two types of man, two worlds. The man of 'self' and the man of 'super-self'. All ye workers for the good of mankind embrace the latter with all his errors, weaknesses or even freaks. But keep away from the former as long as he is stuck to his 'self'. He can learn nothing, he can profit nothing, he can be taught nothing, nothing, nothing. Before you make up your mind to deal with any noble endeavour, first clear the ground (as far as is humanly possible) of every trace of men of this type whatever qualifications or 'fine' qualities they may have, whatever confession their lips may pronounce, whatever banner their hands may raise. 'Do not put new wine into old wine-skins. . . . Do not give dogs what is holy.' And (as Nietzsche would perhaps put it) 'Man—the man of "self" is something to be surpassed.'

Otherwise . . . abandon all hope.

### iii

All that has been said about the contrast between moral obligation and expediency refers to expediency in respect of *the person to whom the moral rule applies*. But this does not mean that the moral rule is not expedient. There is no moral rule without purpose. If it is not expedient to the person who *must* obey it, it is generally expedient to the other people, to the fellow-men of him who is called upon to obey it.

When conscience tells a medical researcher to submit himself to a dangerous experiment, this will not be done for the benefit of the researcher who may, after all, lose his life but for the benefit of the researcher's fellow-men who will profit from his self-sacrifice.

Here I should put forward a proposition of fundamental importance to the treatise. '*Man is the centre of the world of moral obligation.*' There can be no moral rule without aim, or with an aim other than that of serving man. (Not necessarily for the sake of the man who is called upon to obey the rule in a particular case, and who may be sacrificed, but for the sake of others or of mankind in general.) I should point out that the moral rule should serve man in a higher way for the purpose of his qualitative improvement and elevation as we shall see later. But there is no moral rule without aim, there is no moral rule which is not intended to serve man.

Since, therefore, the moral rule is not purposeless, but its main purpose is to serve man, it follows that any moral rule without purpose, and particularly any moral rule that does not serve man, is not a true moral rule. In other words: man may be called upon to sacrifice himself for the sake of his fellow-men but he may not be called upon to sacrifice himself—to suffer any loss great or small—if his sacrifice will not benefit (at least potentially) his fellow-humans.*

Moreover, there is no moral rule *for the sake of God* only. In other words there is no moral law exclusively intended to serve the Divine. Still more, there can be no moral rule hostile to man even if it is alleged to serve God. God has no use for such a rule. The Bible is full of declarations which Paul summarized in his address to the Athenians on Mars Hill. 'It is not because he [God] lacks anything that he accepts service at men's hands, for he is himself the universal giver of life and breath and all else.' (Acts 17, 25). And even what we call our duties to God are really obligations we must fulfil for our sake, for the sake of mankind in general. They are like the duties of children towards their parents (to eat their food, to go to school, to make good progress), or like the duties of a patient towards his doctor—to listen to his advice. Even the commandment, 'love the Lord with all your soul . . .', is not given for the sake of God but for the sake of man. We do not do our duty to serve *His* interests (it would be blasphemous even to think of it). In the last analysis man's duty to God serves as an expedient, a higher or rather the highest expedient for man's benefit.

iv

All I have said before about moral obligation being man-centred leads to this conclusion. *Man has no right to isolate*

---

* There is of course a moral rule not concerned with man. For instance, we must treat animals well. But this is purely derivative. It derives from the moral rule we have accepted about man.

*himself.* A recluse is not a normal type of man. The moral rule is also a rule of sociability. Man lives within the social whole, so his interests and his life should be devoted to the service of that whole. If need be, he may have to sacrifice his life for it. Man as a social animal is not only a fact but also a duty. Man *must* be a social animal. Regardless of the case when man may be called to give his life for the whole, he must so *arrange his life* as to be of service to the whole. This is the first conclusion.

The second conclusion is this. Man must train himself to serve the whole. In other words, man has the duty to try to attain social perfection. How this is to be done is a matter of study and investigation. It is also a matter of education as we shall see later on.

v

There are, however, certain propositions which can serve as guidelines to this investigation.

These propositions are put forward in the form of axioms. Here the term 'axiom' is meant to denote a proposition about man's obligations which he must fulfil if he wants to be really a man. These axioms must be taken for granted. If we disagree about them, it means that we belong to worlds so different that no further discussion on the matter would be of any use.

Four of these axioms, I shall quote here:

1. I think the reader will agree, beyond all question, that sincerity should be the uniting power and the guiding line to man's inner, personal as well as communal life. (Man may also be sincere or insincere to himself.) Of course, there are people who, with the best intentions, prefer not to be sincere and try to tell people things they do not believe because they think it expedient

in the interests, not of themselves, but of the whole (pious fraud, *fraus pia*). Yet, to avoid being sincere on grounds of expediency is nothing but a so-called 'lie for the common good' or a 'conventional lie'. In history, however, there is much evidence of where these conventional lies can lead man. So, what I want to emphasize is that sincerity is not a matter for discussion but the foundation of any discussion.

On the other hand, I do not believe sincerity could be of any harm. Of course, truth should be told with caution, in the proper, instructive, convincing way. It is one thing to tell the truth with caution and another to make caution an excuse for telling a lie.

2. No particular explanation is required about the second axiom: *Freedom*. Freedom is an axiom in the sense that man can be imagined only as a being influenced and dominated by the idea of freedom. One may be a free man even in fetters. Despite what the provisions of the Roman Law said, the slave could well be a free man; but never the voluntary slave. Nor he who would barter his freedom for any kind of consideration. As soon as a man puts his freedom on the scales against material benefits, he becomes a voluntary slave and is no longer a free man. About this there can be no argument.

3. The third axiom is *ascent*. Man has been created to soar high. The Christian precept 'aspire to the realm above' responds to one of man's biological necessities and whoever does not feel this necessity, he is simply not a complete man.

Man is a rising being at least in the sense that he longs and makes every effort to rise.\* He may fail in this endeavour, but he is conscious of his failure. He submits

---

\* This rising trend should not be confused with man's endeavour to improve his position or, as they say, to 'rise in the world'. A completely justified attitude, yet it belongs to the sphere of 'self'.

himself to self-criticism and he is, therefore, a man. Self-criticism is one of the characteristics that distinguish man from the animals.

Man, then, should rise: but how far? There is simply no 'how far'. There is no end of the road to the rising man. Or, if you like, the goal of man's rising is the meeting point with the Eternal 'as far as it is possible for man to be likened unto God' as Plato and the ancient Greek thinkers put it. In any case the axiom of elevation relates to man's advance from the level of 'self' to that of 'super-self'.

4. The fourth axiom is *struggle*. Struggle is the meaning of life. We need not resort to Hobbes and his maxim *Bellum omnium contra omnes*. Struggle does not always mean war or hatred, it also means love, creation and life, not ruin and death. Struggle is the power that makes everything beautiful. If we were to give a definition to death, psychical death, we would say that to die means to give up struggle. And if I was permitted to imitate Descartes, in his famous adage 'I think therefore I am' (*cogito ergo sum*), I would say: 'I strive therefore I am.'

It is obvious how this struggle and the ascent to which we have referred as the third of the four axioms in this investigation are connected with each other. Struggle is good only when it is carried out with ascent as its ultimate goal and motive power. In such case *struggle* already means *ascent*.

On the other hand *ascent* cannot be achieved, or even conceived, without struggle. For such an ascent there are no lifts or escalators. You have to walk up step by step, working your way up, sometimes climbing sheer cliffs without a single foot-hold. And not only you, but thousands of your fellow-men too. How many of your fellow-humans whom you would scarcely deign to notice are spiritual alpine climbers in the struggle of life? It is thanks to them that there are still some remnants of life, true life, in this world!

So man cannot rise without struggle. Nor can he ensure freedom and, still less, sincerity without it. Without struggle nothing good can be achieved. This is a divine law. And, as I said, 'I strive therefore I am.'

Struggle does not necessarily mean war, fighting or coming into conflict with other people. Yet, sometimes it does. In which case, you should not desert your post and retire to your ivory tower. You will fight only if needs must. But then you *will* fight. You will come into conflict with your fellow-men only when this is morally unavoidable. But then you *will* come into conflict.

In this case the struggle will be carried out without a trace of hatred and also with caution. And, as we said concerning sincerity, it is one thing to fight with caution and another to make caution an excuse for not fighting. If you want to be a real man, you must be prepared to offend people if need be. 'Alas for you when all speak well of you.' (Luke 6, 26) This is a great truth. In the zoology of the 'good struggle', a reptile is the 'man' who wants, at any cost, to be on good terms with everybody.

# PART TWO

# Christianity

D

# 5

# Facing Christianity

i

Can one be a Christian today? This question is now commonly heard among Christians of all denominations.

I must confess I do not see why the question is put at all. Why could one be a Christian in the past but not today? What has happened today to justify the question whether one can be a Christian any longer? I could understand the posing of such a question if there had been a revolutionary change in the concept about nature which might shock a Christian believer, as happened when Copernicus or Galileo disproved the traditional geocentric system, or when Darwin wrote his *Origin of Species* in 1859. Yet Christianity has not only survived these shocks, but also manifested exceptional radiance as if it had been stimulated by them. In fact, from 1859 until the end of the Second World War Christianity presented clear evidence of revival and renewal hitherto unknown.

The question could also be justified in view of crimes committed in the name of Christianity such as the wiping out of the American native tribes without any protest from the Church. Then perhaps, the question would not have been out of place. But now, to mention nothing else, with Hitler and his concentration camps and the millions of exterminated Jews still in our minds, now when crimes and acts of terrorism are still committed but no longer in the name of Christianity, how can the question be justified whether one can be a Christian today?

The only honest answer should be this. We ask whether one can be a faithful Christian today simply because today everybody seems to be giving up Christianity. If, then, to renounce Christianity is in vogue today, how can a man or woman who wants to look modern take a positive stand towards Christianity? Can one sail against the tide?

This is what asking whether one can be a Christian today really means. But then it has no meaning at all. It is a stupid question, albeit many books have recently been written about it. Whether the Christian teaching is right or wrong cannot be decided by modernism nor even by the opinion of the majority. And since today's renouncers of Christianity say that the Christian doctrine is wrong, even if it was unanimously accepted by the Europeans of the past, we may reverse the argument and say that the Christian doctrine is *not* wrong even if it is unanimously rejected (which it is not) today. And who knows what is going to be said tomorrow about today's ideas.

Christianity, therefore, is either a delusion of man at all times or it is the truth for man of all times, for the man of today as well as for the man of yesterday and of the past. The stupid question to which we referred in the beginning is not put by those who search for the truth. It is put by cowards who cower before the masses and want to justify their cowardice.

There is, however, something that makes it difficult for modern man to embrace faith, something that should be heeded by the pure and faithful Christians of today. It is the disappointment of the postwar man of today, the man who lives in the period after the Second World War. This is by no means a negligible matter. In its march through the ages, Christianity fought against the Caesars and defeated them. It fought against the wise and defeated them too. But when Christianity has to face man's disappointment in the wrong way it is presented, then it is disappointment that wins and not Christianity.

With this disappointment and the opportunities lost to Christianity we shall deal later. Now we should point out that disappointment is the only reason why the question whether one can be a Christian today is not altogether out of place.

Meanwhile, we should look further into the matter of the legitimacy of faith as was previously examined in Chapter 3.


ii


Religion provides man with an exit through the fence we mentioned in the previous chapters. Such exit is already provided in the four propositions we dealt with in Chapter 2, but only in an incomplete form. These four propositions enable man to, as it were, glance through the fence, while religion proves him with a *complete exit* through it.

We have already explained (Chapter 2, iv) how man feels an indomitable or, I should say, divine urge to climb over the fence we mentioned above. In this respect man is driven by two equally legitimate, yet conflicting, urges which often lead him to a tragic predicament. On the one hand, there is his desire for proof. Man, naturally, requires proof of what he is asked to believe. It is inherent in man's nature to search for proof. On the other hand, there is man's desire to look beyond or rather over the fence, to cross the barrier of known reality into the realm of the unknown of which no proof can be given.

To find a way out of this predicament man resorts to ... illusion. He thinks he can give proof of things which cannot be proved. He thinks he can prove the supernatural (it has been even said that God's existence can be mathematically proved), or (as in the case of the atheistic scientist or scholar of modern times) he thinks, or rather he tries to persuade himself and his fellow-men, that he does not cross the 'fence', he does not enter the metaphysical realm, while in fact he does so without even knowing it when he deals with these problems. He says he is dealing with science, when he is in fact dealing with metaphysics without suspecting it.

The Christian religion shows man the way out of this predicament. It shows him how to escape both from the 'fence' and from the need of proof. It provides man with both an exit through the fence and freedom from the need of proof; and it does so by replacing proof by faith, faith based on the belief in the four propositions we saw in Chapter 2, v. Moreover, the belief in other propositions set forth by the Christian doctrine offers a closer insight into the divine element and its relationship with man in the light of the personality of God-Man, thus providing man with a complete *credo*.

Christianity is not only a doctrine, it is also, or rather mainly, a Personality—the Personality of God-Man as He appeared in His human form. His appearance is a historical event characterized by the fact that Christ appeared not only as a man but also as God thus bringing the supernatural element into history. You may reject Christianity, but you may not take the supernatural element out of it. Without that element Christianity would be, as Pierre-Henri Simon put it in his inaugural address to the French Academy, like decaffeinated coffee.

So, whoever wants to adopt a position on Christianity and its *credo* should first adopt a position on the question of the 'supernatural element in history'.

iii

Christianity is a historical religion. It appeared at a time historically determined and presents supernatural manifestations as historical events. To renounce the historical character of Christianity would be quite arbitrary. You may renounce Christianity, but you may not curtail it by depriving it of its supernatural element as a historical reality.

History is full of supernatural events as they are presented in the light of the Christian feeling and of the Christian faith. These events first appear in the Bible and particularly in the New Testament. It is therefore evident that renunciation of Christianity begins with doubting the credibility of the Bible. For one cannot see how Christian faith can be renounced without questioning the historical reality of the Bible and especially of the New Testament. So it is *that* reality which is called in question. In other words it is asked whether the New Testament is reliable as a historical book.

Two extreme views have been and are still being held on this matter. The one is that the New Testament is a book inspired—and according to some people, to the letter—by God. So, as far as this view is concerned there is no question about the New Testament's historical reality or reliability. The opposite extreme view is that all the Bible and the New Testament is a fairy-tale, good perhaps to be told when mankind was still in its infancy, but in any case a myth almost without any historical value. Where the Gospels are full of historical details on the life of Jesus, the renouncing view maintains that Jesus has never existed as a historical person.

The reader will admit, however, that the New Testament has, at least, been written in good faith by reliable men to whom one cannot refuse the confidence one would place in any straightforward and honest man. This is particularly true in the case of the writers of the New Testament, even supposing they are not those whose names appear on the books but others. So I shall admit, beyond any doubt, that the Gospels, or at least their sources, were written by absolutely sincere men. You can question about them anything you like, but you cannot question their sincerity which they sealed with *their sacrifice*. I know they did not die on a throne or with a cheque-book in their pockets and that the writing of these books cost them a great deal in terms of hardships and persecution and perhaps even violent death.

The sincerity of the gospel-writers is also evident to me in the very texts of the Gospels, in the minor details which they contain. For centuries theologians inclined to renounce the fundamental precepts of faith have made it their task to find differences between the narratives of each of the gospel-writers. On the contrary, I think that these differences support the reliability of the narratives. The gospel-writers had not previously got together to decide, nor had they been instructed on what they were going to write. And even if we accept the surmise of the critics, namely that the gospel-writers were inspired by an original text (Urmarkus, etc.), it is certain that they wrote independently.

Particularly in respect of Jesus' death and Resurrection, I have to say two things. First, the Gospels present many difficult points which one does not come upon in reading about the death of great men. Take for instance the story of Socrates' last moments as described in Plato's *Phaedo*. What a beautiful narrative! All that was written there was meant to stress the superiority of Socrates' character. I do not want to cast any doubt on the truth of the narrative, but I say that Plato's description was meant to provide evidence for the defence of Socrates, to refute the charges made against him and to arouse the reader's admiration for the great philosopher.

Socrates is shown as spending the last day of his life in absolute peace and utter serenity expounding to his friends his ideas about the immortality of the soul. When the executioner warns him that by talking continuously he hinders the action of the poison, and that it may be necessary to go through the trying procedure of drinking the hemlock all over again, Socrates retorts that he is prepared to drink it twice or three times if need be. Having finished his discourse, he goes and bathes himself (so much for those who said that Socrates did not take much care to keep his body clean). Then, to show how unfounded was the accusation that he did not respect the 'city's gods', Socrates ended his life by instructing Crito to see that his vow to Asclepius—to sacrifice a cockerel— is fulfilled. Such was the man the Athenians had chosen to sentence to death for impiety!

I have not the slightest doubt about the truth of every detail in Plato's narration, but do not tell me that it is a simple one and that it does not lead the reader to admire Socrates. Now compare this narration with those of the gospel-writers describing Jesus' death on the cross. Here the reader, far from being led into admiring Jesus through fine words and rhetorical figures, finds it difficult to understand Him. Walking to his death is not a brave thirty-three-year-old young man, unmoved and apathetic. On the contrary He is full of agony and His sweat comes down His face like clots of blood. And how

51

difficult things are made by that *Eli, Eli, lama sabacthani*, that is, 'My God, my God why hast thou forsaken me?' which were Jesus' last words in His earthly life! What, pray, was the purpose of putting those terrible words on record? Well, there was simply no particular purpose. The gospel-writers (or those who told them about these events) repeated the words they had heard without thinking whether it would not be more expedient to hush them up, as it is not unlikely that Socrates might have said something which Plato considered it would be better to hush up. And not only that. Outbursts of pettiness, quarrels, misunderstandings among the disciples, severe reproofs on the part of the Lord (like that 'Away with you Satan' uttered by Jesus against Peter), are presented in all sincerity and simplicity, without any reservation for fear lest the reader might be offended.

No, fairy-tales are not made like that. Am I supposed to believe that the men who wrote these things were telling lies in order not only to gain nothing, but also to suffer persecution, or that they were day-dreamers and yet so sober as to puzzle the reader by the objective manner in which they tell their story which they present without the slightest effort to convince us it is true? No, I cannot believe that. The gospel-writers or those who described these events to them simply related what they had seen, what they had lived, without any effort at presenting it in a more beautiful way or making it easier for the reader to believe.

Now I have a few remarks to make on an argument often put up by those who reject the existence of Jesus as a historical personality. Non-Christian writers who were Jesus' contemporaries or lived soon after Him say nothing about Jesus. Why they do not, I do not know. In any case their silence is by no means evidence that Jesus has never existed for, after all, the same writers are silent about Christianity whose existence is evident to anyone. We all know that Christianity was established some time in the past and has existed since then. Why is this fact not mentioned by writers of that time? There is no need to argue. The reason is very simple. These writers did not take the appearance of Christianity seriously. They thought of it as a freak that would soon die out. They could not imagine how it was going to develop. They scorned it as did Lucian in his work *The Death of Peregrinus*.

It is often asked why this or the other writer says nothing about Jesus. But why should they? We, of course, know *a posteriori* what an event, unique in the history of mankind, has been the preaching of Jesus; we who see the whole earth covered with the leaves of the tree which sprang up from the mustard seed that Jesus planted; we, enemies or friends, renouncers or believers, take considerable interest in everything connected with His personality. But to the man of that time, gentile or Jew, Jesus was a person either totally unknown or insignificant. His disciples, scattered in various places all over the Roman Empire, seemed to be a medley of insignificant heretics, foolhardy cranks emerged from the dregs of society, unworthy of being noticed by any serious historian. If the contemporaries of those men could only have foreseen the size of the great stream that was going to spring from the events they were witnessing! But they could not.

iv

The difficulty in believing the Gospels lies somewhere else. The Gospels are full of stories about miracles. Are we to accept these miracles as being possible or not? The

53

answer could be given in much the same terms as those previously used in our discussion about the supernatural, the reality 'above the fence', faith and knowledge.

I can fully understand disbelief in miracles, but I cannot understand those who say they know miracles cannot happen. Why? From where do they derive the knowledge that miracles cannot happen? Because, they say, miracles are contrary to the laws of nature. But what are the laws of nature? Let us recall Hume for a while. They are nothing but propositions we men have drawn out from observation of what usually happens in everyday life. But no one says that miracles usually happen. This is why we call them miracles. They are extraordinary events contrary to what usually happens. There are no natural laws concerning extraordinary events. A miracle is not an object of knowledge but of faith. As I said, I can fully understand anyone who does not believe in miracles, but I cannot share his disbelief. For if he finds it difficult to believe that miracles can happen, I also find it difficult to believe that the gospel-writers were telling a lie. If you try to reconstruct the procedure under which this 'lie' was engineered, you will find it much harder than to admit the possibility of a miracle. Here, of course, we cannot carry out a detailed investigation into every miracle mentioned in the Gospels, but we shall examine only one, the supreme miracle, Jesus' rising from the grave, in other words, the Resurrection.

After telling us about Jesus' death on the cross, all four Gospels mention and describe His resurrection and the various occasions when He appeared to His disciples after He was raised from the dead. Moreover, Paul refers to the Resurrection on many occasions, but especially in the famous passage of his first letter to the Corinthians (I Cor. 15, 9–34) where the basic importance of the event and the preaching of the Resurrection to the whole Christian message is clearly brought out. This importance was particularly stressed by Paul when he concluded his momentous oration to the Athenians on Mars Hill with that preaching.

Here, however, we come upon the first objection. There are those who doubt whether the Gospels contained the story of the Resurrection in their original form or whether it was added later. To be frank I fail to understand what all this means. Are we to suppose that the Gospels ended with saying that Jesus was crucified and that was all? Pardon me, but such an argument seems to me quite absurd if not ridiculous. The Gospels were written in order to bring the joyous message of the Resurrection. It is quite natural to conjecture the intention of the gospel-writers to write about the Resurrection even if, for the sake of order, they wrote about other things first. That the Resurrection was meant to be brought out as the main event of the gospel stories is shown from the fact that all of the four gospel-writers refer to it, although such is not the case with other events in the life of our Lord. For example neither Mark nor John speak about the *Nativity*, but *they all speak about the Resurrection*. For if they were not going to speak about the Resurrection there would have been no reason for writing the Gospels at all. So, it cannot be seriously doubted that the story of the Resurrection constitutes an integral part of all the Gospels. The question is whether the story is true.

I think one could not reasonably doubt the truth of the story if it were not about a miracle. But for this particular characteristic, I do not see the reason why this story should be less reliable than the narration of any other historical event of that time when verification was not so easy as it is now (by reference to the press, etc.). In other words, why believe so many historical writers of that time and not believe the gospel-writers?

But the question is, as I said, that the story is about a miracle and a great miracle at that. And I can understand the person or, if you like, the millions of persons who say: 'I simply do not believe that miracles can happen therefore I do not believe the story of the gospel-writers about the Resurrection.'

Here again we come upon the argument which I use as a basis throughout this work. It is not enough to say that you do not believe, you must also say what alternative you put in the place of what you reject, and then you must either prove that alternative or admit that by nature it cannot be proved. Well then, what position do you take up on this matter? What do you believe as to the writings of the gospels and other evidence bearing out this miraculous event?

The answer of a renouncer would probably be that the gospel-writers simply became the victims of an illusion. They thought they had seen Christ risen from the dead but, in fact, it was their imagination. This has been repeated thousands of times.

You may admit this explanation, on one condition. That you have never read the story of the Resurrection as presented in the Gospels. Read it and then see if you can honestly believe that that story was purely the imagination of men who, after all, had themselves found it difficult to believe in the Resurrection, as they say, and there is absolutely no ground for doubting their statement.

No! What the gospel-writers said about the Resurrection of Christ was not their imagination. If you want to reject the story there is only one thing you can say: That the gospel-writers have told a lie! Why do you not say that?

Well, obviously, because it is not easy to say that the gospel-writers came together to make up a story with so many lies told in every detail. And for what purpose? To become social outcasts, to suffer persecution, to be tortured and put to death, and all this for the sake of a lie that they had invented? Well, I for one cannot accept that this might be possible. We said that before. There are people who find it difficult to believe that miracles can happen. I find it difficult or rather impossible to believe that the story of the Resurrection is a lie. If I am sure about anything in this life, this is that the gospel-writers were sincere people. Of course they told us things which are foreign to our experience. We men of today do not see such things happen. Yes, but if I say that the gospel-writers told a lie, I say something which is *not in accordance* with my experience. For it is contrary to my experience to admit that there have been people who concocted a story like that, only for the pleasure of suffering persecution or even being tortured to death.

I conclude, as there is no point in continuing the argument, by recognizing that we have come to a crossroads. We either accept the Resurrection or we do not. I accept the truth of the Resurrection. Without difficulty? No, with much difficulty because my experience does not help me to accept it. But if I find it difficult to accept the Resurrection, I find it impossible to believe all what is said by those who renounce it.

v

Now we come to another matter concerning the believer, the person who accepts the Bible as containing the revelation of the will of God. I shall remind him of what I said before about the relationship between faith and

57

knowledge concerning matters above the 'fence'. Faith is not knowledge. It does not remove the 'fence'. By revelation we do not become omniscient. Revelation does not increase, let alone maximize, the capacity of human perception. Revelation is a signpost to the super-human realm, not an eliminator of the barriers to human knowledge. We learn about the will of God by the revelation contained in the Bible because we cannot do it through the faculties of the human mind. 'Every inspired scripture has its use for teaching the truth and refuting error, or for reformation of manners and discipline in right living, so that the man who belongs to God may be efficient and equipped for good work of every kind.' (II Tim. 3, 16-17) Here I shall refer to an anecdote told about St Athanasius, the great bishop of Alexandria. One day, as he was walking on the beaches of Alexandria, Athanasius saw a small boy carrying water in a little bucket from the sea to a hole he had dug in the sand. On being asked what he was doing, the boy answered that he was trying to pour the sea into the hole. Athanasius laughed at the boy's simplicity in thinking that he could pour the sea into that hole. And then he stopped and said to himself: 'Well, I am exactly like that boy when I try to make the nature of God go into my little mind.' What was true of a Church Father like Athanasius can be true of any believer, however deeply he may study the Bible.

The opposite way leads to the deplorable condition described by Paul in his first letter to Timothy: 'The aim and object of this command is the love which springs from a clean heart, from a good conscience, and from faith that is genuine. Through falling short of these, some people have gone astray into a wilderness of words. They set out to be teachers of the moral law, without understanding either the words they use or the subjects about which they are so dogmatic.' (I Tim. 1, 5-7)

I will conclude with Paul's admirable words. 'For our knowledge and our prophecy alike are partial, and the partial vanishes when wholeness comes. . . . Now we see only puzzling reflections in a mirror, but then we shall see face to face. My knowledge now is partial; then it will be whole, like God's knowledge of me. In a word, there are three things that last for ever: faith, hope, and love; but the greatest of them all is love.' (I Cor. 13, 10–13)

# 6

## The Natural Way

Connected with the above is also the matter of the Bible vis-à-vis progress. In the past, the Bible was viewed in, as it were, a static way and so it was regarded as an enemy of progress. According to this view, life could not change because it was governed by the passages of the Bible and even of the Old Testament which of course could not change. Whether it was about matters concerning the regime under which people should be governed or about social justice; whether it was about economic matters (such as the notorious question of usury in the Middle Ages), or matters of fashion, the same Bible passages had to be strictly applied to a developing and therefore changing life. This view led to various interpretations as to the proper way life should be lived.

Thus a conservative view of life was adopted by various people who wanted to do 'what their fathers did' in all matters of everyday life even when it came to the point of choosing between using fertilizers in agriculture or not. In the eyes of many people, this conservative mentality, hostile to everything that was new, was tantamount to the Christian faith, as was a 'conservative' to a Christian.

So, if he wanted to remain faithful to the Bible, a man had to abandon any idea of keeping abreast of the times. This meant, of course, that if one wanted to stick to the

Bible or religion one should do so at the cost of progress. Conversely, it seemed that if one wanted progress one should have to sacrifice the Bible and religious tradition so as to be free to adapt oneself to new developments in life without reservation or even without question. As a result, people are now divided into two camps: those who sacrifice progress to religion and particularly to the Bible, and those who sacrifice the Bible to progress or rather to modernism which they identify with progress. Let me say, however, that there is no need for such sacrifice and that the whole matter is the result of a great misunderstanding.

This misunderstanding relates first of all to the meaning of progress and to the positive or negative evaluation of the new vis-à-vis the old. Conservatives regard the new as a negative value and are against it. The so-called 'progressives' regard the old as a negative value and do all they can so that the old may be superseded by the new. I think that both make the same mistake. They make an idol of time in both cases. The first think that the new is bad, because it is new. The second think that the new is good because it is new. In itself, however, the new is neither good nor bad. A new form of life may be better than the old, but on the other hand, it may be worse. After all, old age is newer than youth without, of course, being better. So, progress is a combination of the newer with the better. The former comes by itself. Life goes on whether we want it or not. The latter is the product of conscious endeavour, it does not come by itself. So, the newer is not, by logical necessity, better. But, in any case, it should be better. How can this be achieved?

This is where Christian guidance can play its part so that the new can really mean progress and not regression. But this should be done without any bias and without viewing things in the way we have just described which has done so much harm to civilization and to Christian faith as well.

The Bible is not a textbook of astronomy, geology or physical science. We say this now, but it took us ages of ignorance and persecution against 'errants' and many an indelible blot on the pattern of Christian history to understand this simple truth and accept the picture that science gives us from time to time of the physical universe. Today, science gives us the answer to many questions put in the Book of Job.

What we said about the 'fence' is also true in this case. The Bible not only contains truths of the reality 'above the fence', it illustrates the knowledge of the man of those times about matters then 'beyond', but now 'inside' the fence. And the more the fence retreats the wider human knowledge becomes.

In describing the connection of the Bible with science, we referred to changes in astronomy and geology. The same applies, however, to biology, medical science and science in general and moreover to moral sciences and especially the science of law. But there are also changes in the conditions of every life and in human needs which today are different from what they were yesterday. These conditions and needs should be faced, of course, in the light of eternity as revealed in the Bible, but not under the influence of the letter of the Bible, as Paul says, 'in a new way, the way of the spirit, in contrast to the old way, the way of a written code'. (Rom. 7, 6) Guided by this divine motto we may find the proper way in which a Christian can deal with progress producing, as our Lord says, 'from his store both the new and the old'. (Matt. 13, 52) Thus the ever changing here-and-now of the moment will be lighted by Eternity so that the new may also be better and that the flow of human things may also mean progress.

ii

There are two propositions as to the revelation of God in the Bible. The first is that the Bible contains the divine revelation of truth: the other is that the Bible is the only revelation of truth, the only way through which God reveals truth to man. I cannot see how a faithful Christian can reject the first proposition without ceasing to be a faithful Christian. But I cannot see, either, how and on what grounds one can support the second proposition which says that God reveals truth to man in no *way other than* through the Bible. To the believer the Bible is God's revelation. But it is not the only revelation of God Who reveals Himself to man 'in many and various ways'.

Of course, there is hierarchical order in most of the ways of revelation. And the pre-eminent revelation is that contained in the Bible. But there are also other ways through which God can be revealed. For example we have the revelation through the 'Spermaticos Logos' (accepted also by the early Church Fathers and writers), the Word of God as it was diffused to the searchers of truth before Christ and especially to the ancient gentile philosophers. Even in the tradition of other peoples and civilizations there is some revelation of God. For God has left no people and no civilization 'without some clue to His nature.' (Acts 14, 16–17)

As to science I refer to what I said before. Scientific discussions, conjectures and theories and, still more, metaphysical propositions disguised as science may not be of divine origin. But scientific facts reached at within the competence of science through strictly scientific methods are also a gift and revelation of God. If not, I must accept a source of good other than God in contrast to the declaration made in the Letter of James (1, 17), that 'all good giving, every perfect gift comes from above, from the Father of the lights of heaven'.

In relation to the moral sciences, I should point out that they also help to lead to conclusions which are in fact part of divine revelation. Let me say a few words *pro domo mea*. After all, the development of legal thought is in itself a divine revelation. I may refer, for example, to criminal law and penitentiary science in general (what enormous progress has been made in that field!), tax law, labour law, the recognition of social justice despite the abuse it has suffered through the foolishness of those who ought to have presented it as a divine command and not as an expression of atheistic violence.

With regard to philosophy, I should refer to the words of Paul in his letter to the Colossians (2, 8) 'do not let your minds be captured by hollow and delusive specula-tions. . . .' But I also know philosophy as a valuable helper of both early and later Christian thought. Even when extremely critical, philosophy has been of great help to the Christian thinker because it makes him organize his thoughts and build up sound reasoning instead of being lost in pious nonsense.

### iii

Now I shall conclude this part of the book with a question: reality 'above the fence' notwithstanding, is it Christianity or its repudiation that fits human nature better? Tertullian, a great apologist of Christianity during the period of the persecutions (AD 155–220), said that the human soul is Christian by nature (*anima naturaliter christiana*): was he right?

This question, asking whether Christianity is man's natural way of life, is particularly important because if we give an affirmative answer, then although, in theory, this answer does not completely prove the truth of the Christian doctrine (one may well say that Christianity is an illusion, but it nevertheless has a salutary effect on man), yet it leads to the thought that if Christianity is man's natural way of life it cannot be an illusion. We shall therefore examine the truth of the question which is, in itself, very critical to our investigation, and shall consider Tertullian's words from three aspects:

1. *Psychologically.* I cannot see how one could contest the fact that a Christian—a true Christian and not a man of the 'religious type' whose soul is torn by anxiety —is, psychologically, normal. You may say that he believes in a dream, a chimera, but you cannot deny that that dream makes him happy. The peace that a Christian—a real Christian—feels in his soul, the peace that makes him face life with confidence is, surely, what man naturally looks for. For one thing, it is the best and most natural tranquillizer or soporific. Even, only for that it is valuable. Besides, the faith of a Christian—I repeat, of a true Christian—broadens and improves his mind and makes him look on life with superiority. True, he may sometimes overdo it and face life with too much confidence. And this attitude may cause damage, great damage if you like. But however great that damage may be, it is always less than the benefit derived from psychical improvement.

It is said that, in order to be happy, one should have good health and bad memory. This means, of course, that one should not remember the wrong done him by others because if he does he will lose his peace and happiness while gaining nothing. There is no doubt that this kind of 'bad memory' is mainly based on Christian forgiveness.

2. *Physically.* That the Christian way of life is also physically the most natural can hardly be doubted.

Christian self-control is also a valuable contributor to physical health. I think it is commonplace to say that the control exercised by the spirit over the body is beneficial to the body. Yet this rule is one of the essential elements of the Christian doctrine. (Just think of the drug addict who by becoming a Christian drops out of his bad habit. And still more of the Christian who can never become a drug addict as long as he is a Christian.)

3. *Socially.* It remains to be seen what a Christian (I repeat a *real* Christian) is like as a social being. Is the Christian, as a man of society, on the right way? To make things easier let us reverse the question. Is it good for society to have Christians (real Christians) among its members? The answer is obvious. I think that even the social question would have taken a different turn if society had really been Christian for the most part and if our Christianity had been genuine.

That, however, is where the shoe pinches. All the possibilities described above can happen if 'Christians' and 'Christianity' are genuine. And this is what makes matters difficult. For, to say nothing of hypocrites, there are Christians whose sincerity cannot be doubted but who seem to have lost their way and who live a mad, unnatural life which has nothing to do with proper Christianity. History is full of men of that type. As an example, I refer to the Montanists from whom even Tertullian could not escape.

But, certainly, it is not only the Montanists who are not genuine Christians. I will say again at the risk of boring the reader that a Christian—if he is really a Christian—is one who follows (or at least tries to follow) the way shown by the Gospel. Far from the Gospel are, of course, the hypocrites. Far from the Gospel are also the ill-informed zealots, the religious fans of uneasy conscience, and those who left the Gospel (as though too elementary) to devote their life to 'foolish speculations, genealogies, quarrels, and controversies over the Law' (Tit. 3, 9), 'angel-worship', 'severity to the body' (Col. 2, 18, 23) and the like. Alas, there are so many 'far-from-the-Gospel' Christians of that type brought out on the pages of history both past and present!

# 7

# Thus the Opportunity was Missed

i

From its advent to this day Christianity has held a leading position in civilization, at least in the west. There was a time when Christian leadership was the absolute and supreme ruler of human affairs. At least from the death of Julian the Apostate (363) to the outbreak of the French Revolution (1789) Christianity had almost no rival to its influence on the shaping of western civilization. But even beyond the limits of that period the man of western civilization resorted to Christianity as a leader. Man has never resorted to a leader with more confidence, persistence and self-denial than that with which he resorted to Christianity.

Christianity as a leader governed our civilization in a truly magnificent and decisive way. If one asks what has been Christianity's contribution to European civilization, the answer is that the latter was simply created by the former. Suppose one were to withdraw from the European or western civilization all the cultural elements in modern life due to Christian influence, what would be left of it? One could not deny, even if one wanted to, the wonderful and uniquely magnificent achievements which make up the assets of Christianity. No other system has ever yielded such assets. Unfortunately, however, Christianity has its liabilities too. These liabilities are connected with Christianity's influence on man.

But before we go any further we should make it clear that when we refer to Christianity we do not mean it as a doctrine, but as a social reality, as man sees it practised every day in the life and influence of its exponents. If these exponents present a distorted form of Christianity which is harmful instead of being beneficial, such a presentation becomes a social reality which should be counted as a liability to Christianity. For it is this reality, good or bad, consistent with the Gospel or not, it is this social reality that man will come upon in his life.

An investigation into the way modern man is being shaped by Christianity should begin with a historical review of the past, as far back as the early days of Christianity, the days of the apostles. This review should be made in a spirit of objectivity, since its purpose is not to criticize and accuse anyone but to redress the evil done through the errors of the past and remove all obstacles that prevent the influence of the Gospel from shaping the type of man who will be able to face the problems of our times.

ii

Even the most objective review of Christianity's march in history would reveal a series of main disadvantages or rather mistakes which have had quite a damaging effect.

1. The first mistake is that Christianity started with a *restricted time perspective*. In the early days of Christianity no one could foresee that the Christian influence would have to be exercised on human affairs for a period that would last for twenty centuries and who knows how many more. So this mistake is due to the eschatological views of the early Christians. The idea prevailing among

them was that although they did not know the exact day of the Lord's second coming (Mark 13, 32) it could not be very far off.

The result was that the early Christians considered Christianity, from its earthly aspects, in a limited time perspective and therefore of limited importance as a guide to human problems in the long run. For this reason they did not consider making any systematic or special investigation into them, nor was the life of a Christian shaped in such a way as to enable him to face these problems. One does not care to deal with problems which will soon cease to exist.

Thus, Christianity left man without guidance as to the problems of this earth and of this life. And when, in later times and later generations, the old eschatological expectation began to wane, Christianity, now a recognized leader, was called upon to find a solution to human problems without even being aware of their existence. Yet these problems called for a solution which man had to reach without the help of Christianity, his recognized leader.

2. The second mistake was theology's one-sided *preoccupation with dogmatic controversies.*

There is no doubt that this situation was primarily due to the heresies which appeared from the beginning of Christianity. They were, indeed, a mortal danger to the Church. Sometimes they were even a threat to social order, decency and in some way to mental balance. War against heresies became, therefore, inevitable. Yet it left Christian leaders so much preoccupied with it that they could not find time to deal with man and his problems.

3. The third mistake was caused by a one-sided, excessive, ill-informed and sometimes insincere *asceticism.*

Asceticism, the life of a monk or an anchorite, is a life

holy in its purpose and (if from pure motives) entirely respectable. Nevertheless, a substantial deviation from the original purpose of asceticism has gradually developed, a deviation utterly detrimental to the relationship between Christianity and the average man or woman who lives in society.

Asceticism means retirement from society, beginning with the family, since it is based on celibacy. This means first that the ascetic cannot claim to be the guide of society from which he has retired and which he calls 'the world', and second that asceticism is an exception to the rule followed by the majority of the Christians who have made society their field of action. Yet, in time, asceticism came to be regarded as the proper Christian life while Christians living in society were considered of an inferior caste belonging to the 'world'. The ascetic showed no understanding of the life-struggle and the problems of the society Christian or the Christian family man. The monk who kept vigil in church praying in a night service could not understand the mother who was kept awake all night by her crying baby who might yet one day become a St Basil.

One of the results of this deplorable mentality is that, as long as it lasts, there can be no *understanding of the sex problem* and of its many aspects, particularly as regards preparation for marriage. To the ascetically-minded the only aspect of the problem that matters is the aspect of sin. Thus, the whole question about sex was destined to become the object of a monologue where sin was the only speaker.

4. But the list of mistakes does not end here. The war against heresies gradually drove people to such extremes as *fanaticism* which is utterly antichristian.

Fanaticism can, of course, be seen also in fields other than religion. It can be seen in politics or even in science.

Nor can it be seen only in the Christian religion. There is also fanaticism in other religions and there is anti-religious fanaticism. Here, however, we are dealing with fanaticism as it appeared in the name of Christianity. This kind of fanaticism acted as a deforming element on civilization and wounded deeply the contact of man with Christianity as a leader.

Fanaticism, however, soon reaches the proportions of a crime. For it soon turns into hatred, hatred in the name of a religion of which love is a fundamental principle. 'In a word, there are three things that last for ever: faith, hope and love; but the greater of them all is love.' (I Cor. 13, 13) Yet—and there is no point in mincing matters—the history of Christianity is for the most part a history of fanaticism, religious hatred, bloodshed for religious controversies whose meaning was far beyond those, individuals or peoples, who wallowed in blood in order to defend or attack them.

We shall not dwell on this matter much longer for if we were to deal with it thoroughly we could fill books with what we should have to say. But we shall refer to one point that shows the size of degeneration of Christian life—and, therefore, of man's contact with Christianity as a leader—that can be reached through the transformation of the religion of love into a 'religion' of hatred. In the conscience of the fanatic, hatred is used as a substitute for genuine compliance of man's life with the teaching of the Gospel. It is a sort of tricky way of, as it were, bribing divine justice. It is as if one said to God: 'I cannot offer you a life according to the Gospel but, instead, I can offer you hatred against those who err in the dogma.'

The reason for resorting to this substitute is simple: compliance with the evangelical law of love requires toil and sacrifice, real sacrifice, much sacrifice, sacrifice of property and, if the Christian teaching is to be taken seriously, sacrifice of self, while hatred is an easy way out of the dilemma. Hatred costs very little while it serves one's vanity, satisfies one's lower instincts and selfish inclinations. It is profitable to its nurse in many ways. Persecution against heterodox Christians was usually a very lucrative proposition to the persecutors. Louis XIV, *le Roi Soleil*, of France did not find it necessary to change his life and become truly pious in order to show off as a Christian. On the advice of Madame de Maintenon, he organized exterminating persecutions, known as *dragonnades*, against the Protestants of France, he repealed the Edict of Nantes and set France aflame with religious hatred. At the same time he filled his treasury with the money of the French Protestants. By doing so, *sa Majesté très chrétienne* thought he was on as good terms with heaven as he was with earth, and thus he felt himself free to enjoy its treasures.

5. Another basic historical mistake was that, little by little, the observance of religious rites, necessary to support religious life, was transformed into ritualism very similar to the 'curse' of the Law from which Christ bought us freedom. (Gal. 3, 13) This attitude led to a special kind of mentality which was a revival of the inhuman pharisaic austerity that carried to the Cross Him who had declared that 'the Sabbath was made for the sake of man and not man for the Sabbath.' (Mark 2, 27) This mentality which gradually possessed the minds of many people in Christian history is quite contrary to what our Lord said about the sabbath being made for the sake of man. A civilization, however, built on this mentality is a civilization of the sabbath and not of man. And a Christianity supported by the sabbath ceases to support man.

Moreover, the rule of substitutes is also applied here. Rites are much easier to observe than sanctity of life.

By observing certain rites man thinks he can be on good terms with God, although his life may be quite contrary to what God wants it to be. By paying 'tithes of mint, and dill and cummin' he feels so satisfied that he can overlook 'the weightier demands of the Law, justice, mercy, and good faith.' (Matt. 23, 23)

Conversely, anxiety and agony for the 'mint and dill and cummin' lead to the character of a psychopath and not of a fighter for the 'weightier demands of the Law'.

6. A gross mistake, or rather mistakes, was also made in the social field. Christians did not appear to show even a trace of anxiety for the widespread social and economic inequality observed among men, for the exploitation of the poor by the rich despite the severe warnings of the Bible. In the early centuries this attitude could perhaps be justified because the Lord's coming was expected soon when every cause of injustice would be removed. But later there was no justifying reason. Exploitation of one man by another was left to go on hardly discouraged and, sometimes, encouraged by Christian leadership. Evangelical commandments, such as 'the man with two shirts must share with him who has none' (Luke 3, 11), or facts, such as 'they [the Christians] had never a needy person among them' (Acts 4, 34), were completely forgotten. The position of the weak, the woman, the child, the peasant or the labourer in the family, in work, in the state or in the social structure; and even slavery and serfdom did not concern Christendom and those who suffered from social or other evils sought redress at the hands of others.

### iii

With all these mistakes, therefore, Christianity as a leader lost its contact with man. Not because it did not give him advice, but because it required him to have his eyes fixed, almost exclusively, at heaven. Christianity did not approach man as a being living and suffering on earth, as a being with problems, as a victim of exploitation and oppression. It did not 'go up to bandage his wounds bathing them with oil and wine' as the Prince of Faith required. The exponent of Christianity approached man as a good adviser, or perhaps as a good ascetic, but not as a good Samaritan. In the last analysis, the divine power of the teaching of the Gospel was not turned to account in such a way as to shape, in all seasons and especially in ours, the man who with the power of the spirit would put matter under control. Christianity has not succeeded in giving shape to that type of man. It has not succeeded for a very simple reason. It has not even tried to do so.

A few brilliant exceptions among the Church Fathers and among some later theologians, are just exceptions. We Christians of various ages have not tried to shape the man who would bring matter under control, we have tried to shape the man who would regard matter with contempt. We have not sought to produce the man of earth who would be guided by heaven. We have sought to produce what we supposed to be the 'heavenly' man. At best we were absorbed in looking fixedly on heaven and did not even seek to cultivate man as the bearer of the power of the spirit, by which the problems of this life, this society can be faced here on earth. Being deeply concerned with the love of God we stopped loving man, which means of course that we stopped loving God. 'For, if [a man] does not love the brother whom he has seen, it cannot be that he loves God whom he has not seen.' (I John 4, 20) iv

The mistakes mentioned until now refer to the past. But there have been also mistakes made by Christianity in modern times and especially in the years following the Second World War.

1. The Second World War was indeed an excellent opportunity for Christianity to help modern man find his way. The ruins with which Europe was filled at the end of the war were also ruins of man's self-conceit. Until that time man had been dazzled by the achievements of science and progress and could not turn his eyes to heaven. But now, out of the ruins of the world he emerged in a state of humility, ready to listen again to the Christian message in order to rebuild not only his house, but also his civilization and preserve his very existence. Man was expecting Christianity to make the grand gesture of coming and treating the wounds inflicted on him by the war. But the gesture was never made. Christianity became once again occupied with 'mint and dill and cummin' (Matt. 23, 23), but never with the problems of modern man.

Yet, postwar man was then humble, but he was also clever. He expected much from Christianity. His expectations, however, were never fulfilled; the big step forward was never taken; postwar Christian leadership never made the great achievement of inducing man to return to faith.

Meanwhile the ruins of the war have been replaced by skyscrapers. The younger generation have no experience of the sorrows and humiliations their fathers and mothers suffered during the war. The average man or woman no longer turns his eyes to heaven. All they care about is comfort and good living. At best they are interested in the social question.

Now man lives no longer among the ruins of the war but in the space age. Christian leadership which failed to approach postwar man cannot now catch up with the man of the space age.

2. Instead of being a leader, Christendom is now in the rear-guard. Wanting to be on good terms with the masses, it slows down its resistance to evil and in the end it tries to justify whatever the masses say or do.

To lay down its course it turns to the Gallup Poll rather than to Heaven. Its compass is demagnetized. It no longer points to the pole star of eternity but to the ship's head. But then such a compass is no longer needed.

3. Moreover, the exponents of Christianity have always tried and are still trying to be with the 'mighty'. Even the so called 'Christian leftism' is mostly due to this tendency. At the moment when these lines are being written 'leftism' seems to prevail everywhere in the world. Among many clergymen and theologians there is an 'opening to the left', not out of conviction, but because power is considered the best argument.

4. In ages past there was a tendency of simulating strong attachment to faith where there was no faith at all. Now we see theologians and even bishops cheeky enough to publicly declare their unbelief, but not honest enough to forgo their posts, their stipends or their privileges.

Christianity has therefore, missed the opportunity given it by the ruins of the Second World War. Disappointed in Christian leadership, postwar man sought comfort elsewhere. In mentality, on the other hand, the man of today has nothing in common with the man of 1945. The opportunity was missed. Man is no longer attracted by spiritual messages. The Christianity of our generation has 'missed the bus'. Yet Christianity is being offered a new opportunity, a new bus to catch. This new bus bears the sign of 'modern atheism'.

77

# 8

# When Atheism is a Leader

A wave of atheism is rolling over the globe. *De jure* or *de facto*, atheism has prevailed both east and west. It has become the 'establishment' in the modern era.

Atheism is not, of course, a new thing. But modern atheism presents three characteristics which distinguish it from the atheism of the past.

First, it is, as it were, an uneducated atheism. In the past, atheism was thought to be the privilege of people with some kind of education who could call upon known scholars and pioneers of science in order to support their views. Today's atheist is more or less an ignoramus. To support his views he calls upon pop-singers or film stars. And wrong as it is to lose one's faith because of Darwin, it is certainly pitiful to lose one's faith because of a film star.

Second, today's atheism has been inherited from the past. In order to become atheists, people of past generations had to revolt against the religious education they had been brought up on. By being atheists, modern young men or women just follow the way their atheist parents have shown them. They have inherited their atheism from their fathers and (terrible to say) from their mothers.

Third, the atheism of today is fully applied in practice. The atheists of the past although being such in theory, were, nevertheless, spiritual personalities in practice.

What they practised was in flat contradiction to what they preached. The conduct of today's atheists, on the contrary, is fully consistent with the renunciation of spiritual values which they uphold. They flatly reject, without hesitation, everything that is spiritual. Their behaviour is the direct consequence of their theories.

This kind of atheism is the 'spiritual establishment' of today. It governs mankind spiritually. In the face of this situation what is the reaction of today's Christendom?

In practice, such reaction is manifested in four ways.

The first is compliance with the atheistic spirit. However terrible it may sound, it is a fact that among a good part of today's exponents of Christendom, efforts are being made to go with the atheistic tide and to make a Christianity without God. Theologians of high reputation have even said that in a proper sense a Christian is an atheist and an atheist is a Christian. In this way, going with the atheistic tide is shown to be the proper thing. We must not forget that the slogan 'God is dead', which reminds one of Nietzsche, was proclaimed by modern theologians.

The second way is *panic*. People who want to keep up their faith in God become nevertheless, panic-stricken when they see atheism approach. Even when they protest against the atheistic spread, they do it in a sheepish way as if they wanted to apologize for trying to go against the tide. In their attitude there is complete lack of the militant spirit required in a struggle. Christians of this mentality appear as a weak minority of people who want to 'eat their cake and have it'. In other words, they want to keep their faith without embarking upon a struggle to defend it. They get shut up in their 'ivory tower' until 'the day of wrath' is over.

The third way is to bury one's head in the sand; to ignore atheism or rather pretend to ignore it; to be

79

concerned with petty problems without taking notice of the approaching cataclysm.

There is also a fourth way: to admit that atheism is today's spiritual leader and as such to call it to account.

## ii

It has been said (mainly by Toynbee if I am not mistaken) that we are now living in the post-Christian era. The idea is now widespread that we live in the post-Christian era and that European civilization is governed by atheism. But if atheism is, so to speak, the spiritual establishment of today it is also responsible for the course mankind is taking. Moreover it is high time for Christianity to stop acting on the defensive and take the offensive. For whole centuries atheism has been the accuser of Christianity. The time has come for atheism to be in the dock.

For years the writer has attacked and condemned with unusual severity the deplorable shortcomings and intolerable weaknesses that Christianity has shown in practice. He was the man who launched, in Greece, the slogan 'I accuse the Christians'. This, surely, entitles him to treat atheism with the same measure.

For years we have been witnessing a spiritual decline which has now precipitated an outright downfall. Atheism has been the backbone of this development. See how closely this wide-scale incidence of crime and spiritual suicide is connected with atheism. Faith would have made these things impossible. Without atheism the spiritual downfall we are now experiencing would be inconceivable. Here I want to draw the attention of my readers to certain particular points.

Atheism today is reckless. The modern atheist has not overcome the difficulties present in his theory. He does not realize how difficult it is to support atheism. He takes it for granted. He does not even doubt his atheism. So, he needs first of all to be shaken out of his naïve cocksureness; to view his atheism with a critical eye; to see that things are not so simple; to realize that he may after all be wrong, and that atheism may well be a delusion.

But, you see, the modern ignorant atheist is not even capable of doubting. He does not care about proof. He is not at all embarrassed with the difficulties encountered by agnosticism and positivism in the past. He cannot even argue. He just rejects. He rejects the faith handed down from generation to generation, but he does not take the trouble to build up his own positive theory and see whether it can stand when put to the test. He just shuts his eyes and smokes pot.

And what is there to shake the modern atheist out of his deadly sleep? There is, of course, Christian leadership. But is that leadership today equal to its task?

I would be the last man in the world to resort to unfair criticism but, on the whole, what is Christendom doing in the face of atheism today?

Christendom cowers before atheism and faces it with an inferiority complex. In some cases it even supports it. For we must not forget that the slogan 'God is dead' was proclaimed by so-called Christians!


iii


Fortunately, atheism itself is doing the job which ought to have been done by Christian leadership. For short though the time of its hegemony has been, atheism is working out its own destruction through disappointment.

In the past I often spoke of the terrible damage caused by the disappointment man feels as a result of taking Christian faith the wrong way. It is now time to speak about the disappointment that atheism causes by nature and not, like Christianity, by misapplication.

In this connection there is also a difference between the believer and the atheist, in two points. First, the believer is disappointed because the principles of his faith are not consistently applied to life. By contrast, the atheist is led to disappointment through the consistent application of atheism to life. Second, the believer, being free, admits his disappointment and tries to remove its cause. The atheist, being a slave to his prejudice, does not confess his disappointment. Nevertheless, the disappointment exists and speaks for itself. Disappointment in atheism is, therefore, growing from day to day. And this is natural for the consequences of consistent atheism are simply unbearable. Here, then, is an opportunity for Christian leadership to help bring out disappointment in atheism. It can be done in two ways.

First, Christian leadership can help the atheist to declare his disappointment. For, unlike the professing Christian who is accustomed to self-criticism and to a humble confession of his mistakes, the atheist is not prepared to declare himself defeated. He is a stranger to self-criticism. So he needs to be helped, as it were, to become sensitive to disappointment before he is swallowed up in it. The sooner this is done the better. And the task of the Christian is to hasten the awareness of disappointment so as to make it less damaging. This task is not so hard as it seems. Make the atheist consider what he can expect from atheism, make him frankly and freely admit the realities that he and his fellow atheists refuse to recognize and the results will be astounding.

Second, Christian leadership should help so that disappointment in atheism does not lead simply to a negative but also to a positive approach to the problem. No mathematical formula can be applied here. The

negation of negation is not a position, so it is not suffici-
ent for Christian leadership. Disappointment in atheism
leaves the door open for something else to take its place.
That something should, of course, be the Christian
message, provided it is faithfully, consistently, systematically and boldly presented.

In summarizing, I would say that as long as negation
of Christianity is the 'spiritual establishment' of today,
it is responsible for the present situation of spiritual
civilization. Negation of Christianity has governed our
spiritual civilization long enough to be judged by
history. So, it is now high time it were called to account.

iv

One of the main and exceptionally prominent characteristics of today's civilization is the contrast between
technical and spiritual civilization (*Zivilization* and
*Kultur*). This distinction, first made by Spengler, refers
not only to the present, but also to the past and even to
the remote past. Today, however, the contrast between
technical and spiritual civilization has widened into a
gap. Technical civilization has reached its zenith at the
same time as spiritual civilization is rolling down to its
nadir. As these lines are being written, man has already
reached the moon. By the time they are published we do
not know what other exploits he will have carried out.
And while technology is soaring to awesome heights,
spiritual values are being declared of no use to modern
man. The man of the atomic age makes no endeavour
to produce a spiritual civilization that would match
and govern technical civilization. While perfecting the
machine to the utmost, we do nothing to shape the type
of man who will put that machine under control and

turn it to account. The higher we make our skyscrapers the shallower we make their foundations.

The values of spiritual civilization are withered. Ideals have disappeared in a maelstrom of contempt and sneers. The way contempt is shown for ideals for which so many lives have been sacrificed is a clear evidence of the downfall of spiritual civilization.

On the other hand, sex worship has led not simply to a lenient and humane view on mistakes in sexual life, but to making sex the purpose and meaning of life. But a life with sex as the only purpose is a life without purpose. This is one of the main characteristics marking the downfall of the so-called 'post-Christian' civilization.

And perhaps, modern man who prides himself on being a realist may not be very much concerned about this kind of downfall. But there are other down-to-earth problems which he cannot escape. Drugs, for instance. I do not know what is going to happen to the future generation because I cannot foresee the future. But the spread of drug addiction is such that one may well fear the worst for the future of mankind even from a purely biological point of view. Post-Christian civilization is now shaping the type of man who has made himself a slave to drugs. Man has rolled down to the last step of the ladder. Mankind is on the threshold of degeneration. As Dante put at the entrance of Inferno: 'abandon all hope'. Except, of course, the one hope offered by eternity.

Meanwhile the tangible proofs of degeneration are more and more being felt even by the most thick-skinned. The spread of crime has become one of the main characteristics of present-day civilization. Society has become morally numbed and has not the strength to react against crime. And not only morally. Even the police have lost their interest in protecting life and property. Moved by a kind of deplorable sentimentality, a low-quality substitute for Christian love, public opinion sympathizes with the criminal rather than with the victim. Little by little crime is, thus, setting its seal on today's spiritual civilization.

The ball rolls on. The level of human decline has now reached the mark of 'nihilism'. Nihilism means an outright renunciation of any value, and rule, any guide in the affairs of men. With nihilism, life has no meaning. And a life without meaning is tantamount to death, for the time being spiritual death and later physical death also.

When the spirit is dead, technical progress becomes an instrument of ruin, not of life. Man makes machines he is no longer able to control. And so the machine kills man instead of serving him.

v

The reader may ask whether I really believe we are heading for death; whether I really think tomorrow will be our ruin. Well, then, I do not. Why? . . . Because, as I said before, I put my hope in eternity. When you have rolled down to the last step you begin to feel the urge to go up again. Just as the Greek poet Costis Palamas says:

> *And having rolled down*
> *To the last step of the ladder of Evil,*
> *For the call that beckons you*
> *again to soar,*
> *You shall feel springing up—oh joy!*
> *The wings,*
> *the strong wings of yore.*

The rules of dialectics apply also to eternity. An ebb is always followed by a flow.

Do I believe such a thing can happen? Of course I do.

Why? Because I see a new opportunity being given man after the loss of the one offered to Christianity at the end of the Second World War. This new opportunity is the 'pods' we read about in the parable of the prodigal son (Luke 15, 11–32). Let me explain. According to the parable, the prodigal son left his father and his home and went to a distant country. There, having squandered all he had taken with him from the paternal home, he became a swineherd. Having nothing to eat, 'he would have been glad to fill his belly with the *pods* that the pigs were eating'. It was these 'pods' that made the prodigal decide to return home. A great teacher, these 'pods'. You may be sure of their convincing power. They are the signposts to the way of return to faith which is the only way of life.

In fact, I do not simply foresee that these 'pods', in other words the deplorable situation mankind is found in today, will inevitably lead back to faith. I do not simply foresee this. I can see it happening now. The first signs of return to faith are now evident. Man is already on his way back home.

Yet this story has also its tragic element. The fact is that I do not see only man's return to faith. I can also see that the returning man will be met by disappointment. There is much fear that Christendom will again disappoint those who return to faith. As an example I may quote the 'Jesus Revolution'. Former hippies now return to faith; faith without knowledge perhaps but not without sincerity. Well, then, I fear that Christendom will disappoint instead of guiding them.

Here we have a vicious circle, a deadly vicious circle, a chain of circumstances repeated again and again. Disappointment leads to negation and apostasy. The disappointed man becomes a prodigal. His desertion of the paternal home is again followed by the same sequence of events: hunger, feeding on 'pods', return to faith.

Then relapse to disappointment, followed by apostasy once more.

Will mankind withstand the perpetual recurrence of these events in a vicious circle? I am afraid not. Unless the vicious circle breaks at last. In other words, unless a new Christianity appears, new not in dogma but in quality. This new Christianity is the subject of the third part of this book.

# PART THREE

# Tomorrow

# 9

# Tomorrow

## i

The greatest demand of our age is this: if the man of European civilization begins to return to faith, he *must not* suffer disappointment. Christianity *must not* miss the bus this time. Return to faith, however, does not mean return to the past (the flow of a stream can never be reversed) but to the eternal. If this is made quite clear, there is hope that the 'bus' will not be 'missed'.

To the faithful Christian the good or evil of 'yesterday', 'today' or 'tomorrow', their success or failure depend on their contact with eternity. We are not frightened of 'today' but we judge it freely so that we can overcome it and prepare a better 'tomorrow'. In the same way we judge 'yesterday'. We do not worship it nor yearn for it. Man will not be freed from 'today' in order to go back to 'yesterday'. 'Tomorrow' will be 'tomorrow': a new 'tomorrow'. 'Behold! I am making all things new!' 'Tomorrow' must simply be better than 'yesterday' and 'today'. In terms of faith this means that 'tomorrow' must be more in contact with the 'eternal' than 'today' is or 'yesterday' was. It must, and we hope, we are almost sure, it will. In any case man *must* do his utmost so that this hope may turn into reality; so that 'tomorrow' may have better, truer, more consistent and purer contact with the eternal than 'today' has or 'yesterday' had.

Which man must do his utmost then? The man of

'tomorrow'? Not only he. For 'tomorrow' is being shaped today. Or rather, 'tomorrow' has already begun. It will much depend on what we do today.

Here the word 'man' is not meant in its collective sense. It means each individual man or woman. Complete darkness may be dispelled even by a single light. One faithful man or woman is enough to build a whole future, provided his or her faith is genuine, consistent and pure. The faith of one person may become the light that will enlighten the man of tomorrow. Having made this clear, we come back to our basic proposition. Man's return must be a return not to the past but to the eternal.

This proposition must be admitted by today's Christians without flinching. Concerning the past, Christendom must tell the truth without mincing matters. It is no use telling lies. Whoever cannot believe in truth, he cannot believe in God either.

It should then be admitted straightforwardly that the past, the Christian past has handed down to us errors, crimes and abominations. Earlier in this book (Chapter 7) the Christians were 'accused'. This was only a beginning, a rough outline of the work that has to be carried out systematically so that every evil that has stained and polluted Christian history may be admitted and confessed. If this is done, then we shall be able to convince people of the good that the past has also handed down. For it has handed down treasures as well as abominations, treasures that have to be turned to account, for we cannot live without them.

Man's orientation to the eternal must be made through Christianity. It is Christianity's main task. This means that Christianity can help man only by being a leader and not by bringing up the rear; by being the compass that will keep the ship of mankind on a steady course and not let her be carried along by wind or water. For the ship's head can be located even without a compass.

ii

Having made this clear we can now see the Christian approach to the question of progress. Let us recall what we have said before about this matter. Progress is a combination of the newer with the better. That the new will replace the old is inevitable; that the new will be better than the old is, however, conditional on many things. Old age is newer than youth but by no means better. Whether the new is better than the old depends on man. Progress is a human task which can be carried out successfully only under proper leadership which should be given by Christianity.

On his return to faith, man should find Christianity occupied with this task.

Our conclusion is, therefore, that Christianity neither ignores progress by persisting in a barren conservatism nor does it believe that progress can be made by itself. Christianity considers it its mission to help and guide man so that the constant flow of human affairs may coincide with their improvement.

Take, for instance, progress in science. How should new findings in the field of science be turned to account by Christianity? This is a matter of enormous importance which Christians should face boldly. The image of the universe given us by science since the time of Copernicus to this day is quite different from the image mankind had known before him. Now man knows that the earth, far from being the centre of the universe, is only an infinitesimal part of it. Man looks at the universe—or rather at part of it—through powerful telescopes perfected to the utmost and his mind reels at what he can see. And the believer stands in awe before the Creator, not only of the earth but of an enormously greater Universe, to Whom the words of the Psalmist now sound even more appropriate 'Oh Lord, how manifold are thy works! in wisdom hast thou made them all.' To think that the earth is only a negligible little star in the domains of Heaven makes you feel humble. But how still more so you feel when you try to deal with matters concerning the Creator and His Creation; when you try to follow the divine path that leads from the God of Israel, the the God who rules 'to the ends of the earth', to God the Ruler of the Universe, a universe that takes billions of light-years to cross and that only in part. Then how can you help asking yourself: 'Can it be that all this great universe, with its innumerable galaxies billions of light-years away, is made of inanimate rocks and stones and that only this negligible particle of the cosmos which we call earth contains life and rational beings?' If not, what tremendous philosophical problems would arise!

The reader has already been told that our intention is not to carry out theological research. But we must say this. Progress in the scientific concept of the universe leads us to an enormously magnificent idea about the world and its creator, an idea that calls for humility that any man should feel when he deals with realities 'above the fence'. Here man, and more so a believer, can do nothing but express his admiration and awe by which he feels himself overwhelmed. This awe and admiration is nothing new. New is, however, its intensity.

### iii

Progress in morality should also be duly regarded. In the light of such a progress Christianity must endeavour to save man. Of course, it is hard to speak of moral progress in our times when technical civilization has reached its zenith while spiritual civilization is rolling down to its nadir. Yet we must admit that the man of our times is more sensitive to moral obligations than the man of the past has ever been. Morality for the man of the past was strictly confined to the sexual sphere. For the rest he was satisfied with the observance of rites and formalities which he used as a substitute for honest living. This attitude led to the emergence of *homo religiosus*, the type of man we described in Chapter 7, the man who, being absorbed in a formal 'religious' life, did not seem to care much about morality in the broad sense, about honesty and good faith in everyday trans-actions and above all, sincerity and purity of intention. Well, for all its spiritual decline, our generation is in many respects more sensitive to over-all morality, than were past generations. This is certainly a sign of progress that future Christian leadership would do well to turn to account.

'Tomorrow' will, no doubt, bring about new living conditions and new social patterns for future Christian leaders to consider and adapt themselves to. Of course, they should adapt themselves to the needs and not to the desires or whims of modern man, with a purpose to lead and not to be led.

Special attention should be given to man's demand *for social justice*. Although purely Christian, this demand has mostly been ignored by Christian leadership. It was only after it became the object of class struggle, creating a great deal of unrest and strife throughout the world, that Christian leaders decided to deal with it, not as leaders, but as submissive followers, out of their desire to protect their interests rather than to obey the commands of Heaven.

Tomorrow's Christianity should, however, deal with these matters not as a follower, but as a leader of the masses. As a leader who shows the way in the light of Eternity. Without the pursuit of *social justice* no genuine adaptation to the eternal could ever be achieved.

Justice, and therefore, social justice, is a heavenly command as well as an earthly demand.

iv

*Faith* is indispensable to the man of the future as much as—or rather more than—it was to the man of the past. Although indestructible and unchangeable throughout all ages, faith is presented to a man who changes from generation to generation. Tomorrow faith will be the same but not man.

Unlike the man of 'yesterday' or, generally, of the past, the man of 'tomorrow' or of 'today' is, in a deeper sense, an adult. Not only the lapse of time, but also the volcanic upheavals, tragic realities and revolutionary changes which took place in the past and are still being enacted, have made him grow into maturity. The man of the past, the European of the Middle Ages and, later, of the period of the Enlightenment was characterized by the inconsistency and instability as well as by the simplicity of an infant. The man of today (and more so, the man of tomorrow) has grown up. He is no longer simple. He finds it hard to believe and if he does, the scope of his faith is very limited. On the other hand, his word and his confession of faith is of more value and carries more weight because it is the faith of an adult. He believes, being fully conscious of the fact, although nothing forces him to believe or rather because he strove hard in order to believe. Those who would have faith govern the new era should know this. The man of the new era is no longer an infant. He is a grown up, mature man. And as such should faith treat him.

Moreover, modern man expects much from believers. He expects them to be consistent with what they profess to believe, and he is prepared to judge them severely if they are not. 'Prove your faith by your deeds' is his slogan. Those who really care about the appearance of a living Christianity in the future should bear this in mind.

As was stated before (Chapter 1) faith should be accepted without coercion, direct or indirect. Otherwise, it cannot be genuine. Faith should be accepted without fear; not even for the fear of becoming a social outcast; not even the fear of God. As was stated earlier, the believer should not believe in God because he fears Him, but he should fear God because he believes in Him. Faith without coercion comes first. The 'fear of God' is its product.

Faith should also be the outcome of a long process that takes place in the soul of man. Man will *doubt* when he doubts and will *believe* when he believes. It is only then that faith will support life instead of asking to be supported by it.

I will remind the reader of what I have said about doubt (Chapter 3, vii). It applies, to a greater extent, to the Christianity of 'tomorrow' and to man's return to faith. To many this return will be manifested *per saltum*, at a single bound, by a sudden turn from unbelief to faith. To some others, however, the way back to faith will have to cross the region of doubt. The unbeliever will begin to doubt about his unbelief. This doubt is not yet the happy ending; it is, however, a hopeful beginning.

One of the main tasks of the Christian of tomorrow will be to turn this hopeful beginning to account. He will also have to deal with the doubt of those believers whose faith has been shaken by the bleak winter of widespread unbelief around them.

Now, referring to what I said about agnosticism I would add this. The man who will decide to return to faith will be a mature man. He will, therefore, not expect the believer to know everything.

97

A child usually expects his parents or teachers to give an answer to any question that it may put to them. It expects them to know everything. An adult, however, makes no such claims. However clever or learned he may think his fellow-man to be, he does not expect him to be omniscient. What he expects him to do is to tell the truth about his personal beliefs and not to give an answer to every question he may be asked. An adult does not think much of any man or woman, however learned, who speaks *de omni re scibili et quibusdam aliis*.

The same thing happens when an adult turns to faith. He does not expect faith to satisfy his curiosity about everything; he expects it to give him support and guidance. The believer will not be expected to express himself in highfalutin' language; he will be expected to lead a life consistent with his principles. He may often have to admit that he does not know, just as Paul said once: 'I have no instructions from the Lord.' (I Cor. 7, 25) But he will have to be sincere and consistent with what he says.

Sincerity and consistency in faith is renewed through struggle with the environment. As far as faith is concerned, man is as it were, winter-bound. And so will be the man of tomorrow, at least in the beginning, when he decides to return to faith.

# 10

# Being Up-to-date

### i

Now, I want to deal, more extensively, with the matter of 'up-to-date Christianity' because we must know what we mean by it today and what this term will mean tomorrow.

This question refers, first of all to faith and its content, or to the dogmatic aspect of Christianity. Should we believe what our fathers used to believe in centuries past or should we change the content of our faith and adopt it to the thought, mentality and tendencies of our time?

The question is by no means a new one. It goes back to the eighteenth century, if not before. In the nineteenth century, to say nothing of earlier ages, a kind of 'modernism' in faith, in dogma and in theology appeared on the scene. Now, with the twentieth century coming to its end, this 'theological modernism' is becoming more and more widespread. Although expressed in various ways and by various schools, this tendency was initiated by a unanimous desire for compromise. The modernist who followed this trend was a compromiser. He saw faith deserted by the masses, but he did not want to lose contact with them. And so he thought he could facilitate things by making some concessions. So he sacrificed the eternal element in order to follow modern man's ideas about Christianity. He thought that the masses had no use for the supernatural any longer, and so he cut off

99

from the Gospel now one thing and then another until at last he had removed from it everything that was connected with the supernatural. Having done this, the compromiser set off to meet and attract the masses with this sort of 'non-supernatural' Gospel. (Now what a 'non-supernatural' Gospel would be like is more than I can imagine.)

But instead of meeting the masses, he met . . . a compromiser of another kind. This compromiser came from a point diametrically opposite to the starting point of the first. He came from the renouncing camp, from the camp of materialistic and anti-Christian negation. He also wanted to attract the masses. And, therefore, he thought he could do with some concessions. Christianity, he thought, should not be attacked all at once. 'Christianity,' he said, 'why, of course! Just take this away, cut that off, don't insist on admitting the supernatural element and then. . . . why, we become Christians too!' No wonder that the slogan 'God is dead' has been put up by compromisers of this kind. They are the atheists who claim to be Christians.

So this 'clever' renouncer and compromiser who knew very well the power of Christianity, even as a name, set off to meet the masses. Thus starting from two different points, the two compromisers, the 'modernist' and the 'clever' renouncer met each other half-way. The meeting was such as to make it impossible for those who read their works to tell the 'Christian' who makes concessions from the renouncer who does not want to strike suddenly. Still, there was yet another point where these compromisers met: the error they made as to the point of their meeting. They thought they had met in the soul of the people. In fact, however, the meeting point was in the wilderness of insincerity and conventionality miles away from the people's soul. For the people's soul cannot be deceived by such camouflaged ideas. If Christianity is not the voice of Eternity, it is nothing. The 'common man' of today knows this far better than the various exponents of theological and dogmatic modernism think he does.

This inconsistent, insincere 'up-to-dateness' that makes concessions at the expense of faith for fear of shocking modern man and in order to flatter him, is utterly purposeless. Things speak for themselves. For if tomorrow, the 'pods' of unbelief begin to tell on man he will turn to the real, unmaimed, uncompromising faith in the eternal; in the supernatural; in God. He will turn to faith in an unmutilated Gospel. This is why 'dogmatic modernism' is something false and, as we said, utterly purposeless.

ii

The problem, however, has not only its dogmatic aspect. It is also a problem of faith in modern life. For life itself should be now and still more tomorrow an integral part of Christianity. This must be more and more emphasized. Christianity is not *merely* a dogmatic or ethical doctrine. Christianity is life, the life of men and women who lived on this earth in times past, who are living now and who will live in the future. It is a chain of generations which come and go and which are components of Christianity, contributing to it their being, their traits and their special characteristics of place, time and living conditions. Christianity is not only eternal, it is a synthesis of the eternal and temporal elements. Thus Christianity has in it the earthly and human element which depends on human conditions relating to place and time. Faith is one eternal and unchangeable. But the human expression of faith in the life of the faithful has its variations which Christianity uplifts without killing them.

In this aspect our modern era expects to see the new Christianity.

Thus, for all the one, eternal and unchangeable faith that integrates, Christianity, as an expression of life, has its variations which distinguish the Christian of the catacombs from the Christian of the fourth century: the Christian of the Middle Ages from the Christian of our generation; the Christian of today from the Christian of tomorrow or of the future. On this human side, Christianity has a history, that is, a differentiation in time. In this human aspect, Christianity differs today from what it was yesterday and will differ tomorrow from what it is today. Let us see some of the numerous instances where this up-to-dateness could be manifested, just to help the reader gain a clearer insight into this important matter.

I shall begin with the difficulties, needs and problems and even sufferings which beset man of this age. But will the man of tomorrow encounter difficulties, needs or sufferings? Would it were not so! But no doubt he will have problems and manifestations of sickness and failure. And if Christianity does not help man to face such problems, and overcome sickness or failure then . . . it will once more miss the bus.

But in order to help his fellow-man, the Christian must prove in practice that he is not a stranger to society but an integral part of it. Like the good Samaritan he must see the wounds of modern society not just to go past, but to go up and 'bandage' them, 'bathing them with oil and wine' which, of course, he must produce himself from his faith and not borrow them from the patient. This is not being done today and this is why Christianity misses opportunities. It must, however, be done tomorrow at any cost.

Thus, in modern society, the Christian should be the messenger of eternity who will give the world slogans, not take them from it. He should come, not as a stranger to, but as a member of society, flesh of its flesh, as one who shares the same problems and the same anxieties but faces them through the power of eternal faith.

It is quite clear that this sort of 'synchronism'—the dealing with the problems of today, their understanding and solution through the power of the Gospel—must not be simply of a general character. It should be thoroughly specialized because when it comes to application to particular cases there is differentiation in time and need for synchronism.

For instance, crisis in the modern family and preparation for the family of tomorrow will not, of course, be faced by making concessions at the expense of eternal moral values. But it will not be faced by generalities either. Like a thoughtful researcher, with zeal prompted by love, guided by the light of his faith, the Christian will have to consider the modern family, which is not like the family of yesterday, and also the family of tomorrow which will have to be guided by the light and the power of eternity.

The modern Christian family is an expression of up-to-date Christianity. The family is just one example. There are many others such as professional orientation; modern dietetics; the problem of recreation which the tired and nervous man of today needs as much as he needs food (and yet the type of recreation he gets is almost like giving salt water to one who is dying of thirst); the problem of spare time of which modern man has plenty under today's working conditions. I will also refer to other problems that today's Christianity has failed to face with success. (But it cannot afford to go on failing.)

There is, first of all, the problem of social justice. Christianity has made an awful mess of it. For whole centuries Christian leaders—albeit not every Christian in particular—had ignored it. And when they decided to deal with it they did so not as leaders but as followers of the now powerful masses. Tomorrow's Christianity will be called upon to face, in the light of eternity, the social problem as it will be tomorrow and to apply the eternal laws of justice to the society of tomorrow. To do this today is now too late.

Then, there is the problem of feminism. Here Christianity has blundered again. For ages 'men have been the lawgivers who made laws against women'. Today the problem of feminism is in a state of chaos. Tomorrow Christianity will be called upon to prove that it can draw light and power from the treasury of eternity in order to show the right course to be followed.

There is, also, the racial problem which bears a resemblance to that of feminism. To be frank I have not quite studied the problem. In my country it is as yet unknown, but I fear that what I said about feminism applies somehow to the racial problem also.

Last but not least comes the problem of the younger generation. Being, in the past, under the yoke of their elders, young people have now revolted. But they have not found the Way yet. They must be told the truth by someone who knows it. Today Christianity provides them with flatterers. Tomorrow it must provide them with guides and leaders who will show them understanding and love; who will tell them the truth, however bitter it may sound; who will approach them in order, not simply to win them over to their side, but to give them real help. If the younger generation want to be flattered let them be reminded of the answer Phocion gave to Antipatrus: 'Thou canst not have Phocion as thy friend and at the same time thy flatterer.'*

The task of an up-to-date Christianity is to bring modern life and today's problems into contact with eternal, indestructible and omnipotent Faith.

* Plutarch, *Agis and Cleomenes* II.

This is the only guarantee that man's life—a life worthy of being lived by human beings—will not end on this planet no matter how hard negation is trying to bring it to an end.

### iii

The term 'up-to-date', as it was meant previously, should also have reference to the 'Christian altar'. By this we mean, first of all, public worship. But we also mean private or family worship—where it still exists—and, generally, spiritual meditation as exercised by a believer.

In a sound modern society, the altar should be an object of respect. The altar belongs neither to the past nor to the present, it belongs to eternity. What Plutarch said about this is true in all ages. You will never see a city without 'holy places'. Cities are now built, of course, intentionally without altars. But this is purely artificial and spurious. A city without altars is a city without freedom, without spiritual civilization. Man will need the altar tomorrow as much, or rather more than he needs it today. The altar is the symbol of the eternal and unchangeable element in the march of time. It is, however, necessary that due regard should be had to the requirements of modern man in each age—especially of the 'grown-up' and exacting man of tomorrow—as regards worship.

In this sense, worship should be up-to-date. It must appeal to a grown-up man who knows what he is doing, why he is doing it, what is happening and why it is happening at the time of worship. The sentimental aspect of worship should not of course, be rejected. For all I know, the man of tomorrow may be more sentimental than the man of today or of yesterday.

Moreover, every believer should be given a chance of

actually participating in worship. Still more, piety—in the sense of orientation of human thought towards the eternal—should be revived, so that modern man may keep his contact with the eternal without ceasing to be up-to-date. And if I may be permitted to borrow from the history of law the term *usus modernus pandectarum*, I would coin a new term, the term *usus modernus pietatis* (modern use of piety) to mean that tomorrow there will be expressions of piety which, while not differing in substance from similar expressions in the past, will, nevertheless, put into practice the words of Plutarch (*Life of Pericles*) who calls for the substitution 'for timorous and inflamed superstitition [of] that unshaken reverence which is attended by a good hope.' Such expressions of piety will be adapted not to the whims or freaks but to the real needs of the 'grown-up' man of tomorrow with respect to worship.


iv


Now I will say something which will, perhaps, offend some of the readers more than anything else I have put into this book. The Church cannot possibly lead tomorrow's man on the course of his life with the clergy as a profession. Today the office of a clergyman, instead of being a ministry, has become a 'job', sometimes very profitable. However profane this may sound, it is true, since clergymen use their office as a means of earning a livelihood.

Well then, this situation should not be allowed to continue. The Church needs ministers who will follow the example of St Paul, who would be ready to sacrifice themselves for the Gospel, not make a living out of it. Christianity will again become a leader when her ministers earn their living from an occupation that has nothing to do with their ministry as clergymen; when they look on the Christian work as a sacred duty and not as a means of earning a livelihood.

This may sound utopian but it is not. In the first place one cannot deny that the freedom of the Christian ministry from the bonds of a profession is one of the conditions for Christianity to become the leader of tomorrow's society. If the clergy ceases to be a profession there will be no longer any financial problem in the Church. The problem of Church property will be solved only if the Church has no need of property. Only then will the Church be able to speak to the destitute of tomorrow, when it will be able to repeat the words of St Peter: 'I have no silver or gold.' (Acts 3, 6)

Besides, recent developments in the social pattern have made things easier. The successive reductions now made in working hours and in the retirement age of public or private employees will facilitate the effort (if there is going to be such an effort) of the Church to recruit her ministers from people of mature character; who have proved their worth in society; who earn their living from an occupation outside the Church; who are prepared to offer their services to the Church with zeal and without any remuneration whatsoever. You may well doubt whether there are any such people today. The doubt is justified but not decisive. Or perhaps it is not justified after all. For we shall never know the results of such an endeavour until it is actually made. In any case, we have many encouraging examples of voluntary dedication to charitable work.

We do not expect a sudden change to take place overnight. But a start should be made, in any case, so that the Church may be restored to a really leading position. Some lower posts in the Church may perhaps be occupied by people who will make a living out of them. But, on the whole, church ministry should be looked upon as a challenge to engage in a contest of sacrifice and not as a means of earning a livelihood. Church leaders should be men who have succeeded in other walks of life and who should earn their living from sources other than the Christian work which to them should be a matter of 'give' rather than 'take'. Christianity will again become a leader when it again becomes a matter of sacrifice; when those who lead are prepared to sacrifice themselves in order to defend their faith and not to surrender to the 'mighty' of the day.

By sacrifice we mean not only the sacrifice of life which after all, is not always required, but also the sacrifice of interests, intentions or ambitions. A Christian should live in a spirit of sacrifice, 'counting everything sheer loss', so that the Christian message may turn into reality. A Christian is not one who makes a living out of Christianity, but one who sacrifices himself to it.

This is indeed 'a hard saying', yet it must be said if we want to speak frankly and plainly. If Christianity does not ensure among its followers a spirit of sacrifice, it will again be missing a new opportunity and the vicious circle of which we spoke earlier will work again. But if it does ensure that spirit, the opportunity will no longer be missed. Another bus will be coming along. Christianity will only have to see that it does not miss it this time.

# I I

# The Fruits

### i

There is a passage in the New Testament that the common man, even (or, rather, more so) the unbeliever, has heeded more than the faithful, pious Christian people and leaders have ever done. It is the passage when the Lord speaks of the fruits as a criterion of the genuineness of a person's religiousness. 'You will recognize them by the fruits they bear,' He says. (Matt. 7, 16)

As stated earlier, the fruits of Christianity are the type of man, the perfect type of man, which it can produce. It is this type of man through whom Christian faith is, as it were, legitimized. In order to believe, people today look for something tangible on which to support their faith. They can no longer say like John: 'We have heard it; we have seen it with our own eyes; we looked upon it and felt it with our own hands; and it is of this we tell . . . the word of life.' (I John 1, 1) A span of two thousand years separates modern man from the miracles of the New Testament in which he is asked to believe and not—like the eyewitnesses of the life of Christ—to use them as a means of upholding his faith. Modern man is now too mature to believe without something to support his faith. That something is the type of the 'perfect man' presented as the 'fruits' of Christianity. If this type of man is shaped by Christianity, no reasonable person will ask for the proof of things that are not susceptible to any proof. If Christianity fails to shape this type of man, no 'proof' will ever be capable of supporting faith.

ii

Thus, Christianity must needs produce this type of man. At least tomorrow since today it is, unfortunately, too late. But in order to produce him, Christianity must first 'design' him. For now it is not clear even to Christianity what such a type of man should be like. In fact no one outside Christianity is trying to deal with such a design. This is why man totters on the road of his life. This is why spiritual civilization cannot stand. Man either falls into a morbid religiosity and becomes the 'religious' man we saw before or abandons faith completely, turns his back on God and gradually (sometimes not so gradually) ceases to be a human being.

The task of designing the type of the 'perfect man' is however, not easy. It involves a thorough study of human affairs, in faith and in knowledge about the man of today as he is. And not only as he *is*, but also as he *should* be. We need a new kind of anthropology, guided on the one hand by the eternal and, on the other by present reality. An anthropology of this kind will not issue directives without knowledge of reality, nor will it be a slave to reality, with the idea that because man is what he is, he should, therefore, *be* what he is: it will form a design of what man should be.

We need a kind of 'deontological anthropology', that is, one to combine the command of Heaven with the conditions of everyday life. Without this there will be no end to trouble.

In this leading endeavour Christianity should, of course, be inspired by Heaven, but it should also consider earthly problems. Until now, Christianity's only concern was, at best, to imitate the angels. But as Pascal put it, '*Qui fait l'ange fait la bête.*' As stated earlier, Christianity has not tried to shape the man who would put matter under control; it has tried to shape the man who would regard matter with contempt. This definitely has to stop.

Now, the task of Christianity is to give shape and guidance to the man of today or rather to the man of tomorrow. The great figures of a twenty-century-old Christendom (and also of pre-Christian civilization) will, of course, be used as an inspiration but the main course will be laid down for the man of today, or rather, for the man of tomorrow, the man of the twenty-first century, of the third millennium after Christ. We need not dwell longer on this matter. We simply refer to what was stated earlier about 'up-to-date Christianity'.

### iii

Needless to say, a Christian should be a man of virtue. Virtue of course, includes piety but it does not confine itself to it.* It is rather a combination of all the good qualities expressed by the ancient Greek term ἀρετή. It denotes all the learning and equipment that man needs in his struggle on this earth and in this age. If I may put it this way, it is the virtue of fighters.

---

* *See* Plato, *Laws* A 631c: 'And wisdom, in turn, has first place among the goods that are divine, and rational temperance of soul comes second; from these two, when united with courage, there issues justice, as the third, and the fourth is courage.' (Bury's translation); and

Aristotle, *Rhetorica* A, 9, 3: 'The components of virtue are justice, courage, self-control, magnificence, magnanimity, liberality, gentleness, practical and speculative wisdom. The greatest virtues are necessarily those which are most useful to others, if virtue is the faculty of confessing benefits.' (Freese's translation)

A man of the 'religious' type mentioned before looks for what he thinks higher things and neglects those which are fundamental, the basic virtues which society expects him to show. He is like a student of mathematics who, trying to learn the differential calculus, forgets all about the four rules. A Christian should begin from the basic virtues. First, he must be *just* in the sense of practising elementary justice and obeying the laws. He must also be sensitive to social justice, which is a completely different thing from political convictions and aspirations. But in any case man's perfection should also refer to his quality as a *social* person.

I shall now refer to the known classification of virtues into 'male' and 'female' ones. For example 'valour' is considered a 'male' virtue and meekness a 'female' one. Yet both are needed and wisdom will tell when to use the one and when the other.

In any case this virtue must also be a virtue of power. For ages now society has identified virtue with weakness. It is high time the virtuous man appeared 'by the power of God'. It is high time that the man of virtue, piety or religious faith ceased to be identified with the anxious, unbalanced, sulky specimen of humanity that appears in society as an example to avoid rather than to follow. In one word, the Christian of tomorrow should be of an imposing personality, fully equipped with virtues so as to set an example to modern society in which he will appear as a leader. This was hardly heeded, if at all, by the Christianity of yesterday or of today. Tomorrow, however, the Christian should appear as a fully integrated personality.

Love, is no doubt, the crown of virtues. In his first letter to the Corinthians (Chapter 13) St Paul gives a magnificent description of Christian love. But who remembers today what the Apostle has said about it? 'There are three things that last for ever: faith, hope and love; but the greatest of them all is love.'

Two thousand years have passed since he wrote these words and during all that period much has been said and done to blot them out. This is being paid for now and very dearly. So, the pre-eminence of love should again be established. Otherwise we shall never see a live Christianity.

Here let me give you an illustration. Our soul is like a ship moored with two ropes: 'Faith' and 'Love'. Well then, if one of these two ropes is to carry away let it not be 'Love'. For one who loves will no doubt nurture some kind of faith, while faith without love is satanical. 'The devils have faith like that, and it makes them tremble.' (James 2, 19) Without faith love gets tired: without love faith is tantamount to blasphemy.

Moreover, referring to the distinction made before between male and female virtues, I would say that love has become a female virtue identified with sentimentality or weakness. So, little by little a separation has developed between love and power. Those who have love, have no power. And those who have power have no love. This separation must give place to a synthesis. A synthesis that will be the key to success.

A powerful love, enthroned in the soul of a fully equipped personality and guided by faith cannot but lead to internal *peace*. Whoever possesses that peace will have nothing to envy in the tranquillity of the Stoics. So a Christian should be first of all a man of justice and, above all, a man of love. These two supported by faith will bring about the much coveted internal peace and tranquillity. Without these three principal virtues no other virtue can have any meaning.

iv

The problem of the younger generation, almost unknown in the past, has now become the most crucial problem in our civilization. The problem affects not only the present, but also the future. Today it has caused a sudden upheaval in social institutions and spiritual trends in our age.

In the beginning 'angry young men' got furious about everything and everybody. They accused their fathers and all earlier generations; they cut off the connecting links joining one generation to another and created a gap between themselves and their fathers and, still, more their forefathers. It is true that these angry young men have not made it clear whether they realize that the same gap may exist between themselves and their children when they, the young people of today, grow old. In any case the generation gap is now a reality that causes a lot of problems today and creates an unhappy feeling about the future.

The situation becomes even graver as this gap is not confined to generations, but it extends to traditional ways of life, institutions and sacred legacies. All these are being mercilessly pulled down by the younger generation who never stop to ask what they are going to build in the place of what they are pulling down. 'Today we are pulling down,' they say, 'tomorrow we shall think about what we are going to build.' But they do not seem to realize that tomorrow it will be others who will have the privilege of being young.

Of course, not *all* young people are 'angry', nor do they *all* pull down. Yet the generation gap and the pulling down of traditions and institutions is a reality caused by the decline of spiritual civilization mentioned earlier. Thus, although the 'angry young men' are a minority, spiritual decline is universal.

The results of this decline are, of course, hardly encouraging. Who is then to blame for this situation? The young people or their fathers? To answer this question one should take time to deal with the causes of this decline. This has extensively been examined in articles published in the magazine *Syzetesis*. For the purpose of this book, however, we may refer the reader to what is stated earlier about atheism. The outbreak of revolt among young people is not irrelevant to the atheism handed down to them by their fathers. If the younger generation is sick, it is because our age is sick. How could it be otherwise in view of the spiritual starvation brought about by materialism of past generations?

v

But instead of trying to find out where the blame lies for this situation let us try to see how the youth question should be faced by Christianity today and more so tomorrow.

Just remember what we said before about man's maturity. This applies also to young people and even to children. Today's young people mature much earlier than in past generations. This must be borne in mind by anyone dealing with the young problem. It is this sudden development of maturity which has caused the volcanic upheaval observed in the modern world. What young people want today is not to be instructed, but to be frankly spoken to. One of the main tasks of Christianity is to speak to young people with frankness; not to flatter them but to help them; not to win their applause, but to impress the truth on their memory. If they do not listen today, they may have something to remember tomorrow when the time comes to resume their proper course.

Young people should be told that their actions should be consistent with their ideas. If they demand their rights as mature personalities, they must also assume responsibilities. If they want now to hold the torch in the relay race of history, they should also accept responsibility for whatever happens. If they denounce what their fathers have handed down to them, they should not only voice their indignation but also create their own new world which will have to be tested by future generations and future times.

When the test comes, Christian faith must appear in a frank, straightforward and sincere manner, without compromise. A very difficult task, no doubt. It may well be called superhuman. Yet, we men and women of today can help by disseminating the message of faith, especially to the younger generation. To this end, the pages of this book may prove to be a valuable contribution. Besides, it is for this special purpose that they have been written in the first place.

### vi

The reader may now wonder whether what is written in this book and especially in Part Three is a mere theory, a deontological theory propounded without concern over practical application or a plan set forth in the hope of its being turned into reality.

Our answer is very simple. Not only do we hope but we are also sure that what we have said here will be applied to life. By this we do not mean that the day will come when masses of people from the four corners of the earth will close the ranks in a world-wide effort to respond to the demands of Heaven and of our age. In fact, what we expect is quite the opposite.

Since the time of Emperor Constantine, Christendom has forgotten the words of our Lord: 'Enter by the narrow gate . . . the gate that leads to life is small and the road is narrow, and those who find it are few.' (Matt. 7, 13, 14)

Boasting of the hundreds of millions of faithful all over the world, Christianity does not seem to understand Christ's concern for the 'little flock' (Luke 12, 32); yet it must. It must understand Him today in order to remember Him tomorrow. For tomorrow's Christianity will have to tread the narrow road and it will be the little, the very little flock.

Tomorrow the Church may, perhaps, be called upon to remember the still harder saying of our Lord: 'but when the Son of Man comes, will he find faith on earth?' (Luke 18, 8) As far as faith is concerned we are, as it were, winter-bound. Around us faith is growing cold. Ours is a wintry Christianity. Sorrow presses heavily on the heart of the faithful and their only comfort is the Beatitude: 'How blest are the sorrowful.' (Matt. 5, 4) The times we live in require the Christian to stand fast to his beliefs and tread bravely the 'narrow road' with the few, or even alone—not because he will be actually alone but because he will not know who his fellow-believers are, where they are and how to get in touch with them. These few will have to bear the burden and assume the task of keeping the Ark above the waters, of tending the light that will disperse the darkness and show the prodigal the way back home.

As stated earlier the 'pods' of the parable will make man come back to faith. So, the few but real believers of today, the 'little leaven' must enter the Ark of Faith and keep it safe, so that when the flood is over and the man of tomorrow sets off on his way home he will be met not by disappointment, but by the light and renewing power of faith; the faith that will turn into reality the Lord's declaration: 'Behold! I am making all things new!' (Rev. 21, 5)

This Ark must prove a bulwark of resistance, a warm spot amidst the cold and bleak surroundings of spiritual winter. All the inmates of this Ark will be heroes, because they will have to go against the tide. As such, they will be called upon to perform the heroic task of welcoming those who, tried in the furnace, now wish to set out on their journey home.

### vii

There may be one or two or many—if not all—of my readers who will say that what I have written about a 'wintry Christianity' the 'Ark of Faith', loneliness and the like is hard to take. But this is what our Lord Himself was once told: 'This is more than we can stomach! Why, listen to such talk?' (John 6, 60) Yet our Lord was perfectly right. His saying was hard because truth is hard. I would not hesitate to refer again to what He said about the prospects of faith: 'But when the Son of Man comes, will he find faith on earth?'

On the contrary, what I fear is that I may be accused of being too optimistic, or rather of being a dreamer. For it is not a logical necessity that the vicious circle to which I referred earlier will be interrupted this time by a revived Christianity that will prevent disappointment. Nor is it *a priori* certain that mankind will withstand another repetition of the vicious circle in its perpetual motion. It is logically possible that Christianity will fail to show the power and revival it must show (such a failure has often been noticed in the past) and that mankind will not endure new disappointments. It is quite possible that, this time, the prodigal will fall headlong into the abyss. This possibility is made even more likely by the astounding progress of technology, which may become fatal if spiritual life is completely dead. In which case who knows what the future holds in store for us?

Moreover, that part of mankind that was called 'Christian' is no longer in the vanguard of civilization. Peoples who do not even call themselves Christian are coming to the forefront. Here, then, the parable of the prodigal seems not to apply. The home that the prodigal has left is no longer a Christian home, and if he decides to return, he will not come back to the Christian faith. So, what will happen?

### viii

To these and all other questions reflecting man's anxiety about 'tomorrow', the writer has only one answer to give. His answer is to refer the reader to what he wrote in the first chapter about the 'fence'. These things are beyond the knowing capacity of the human mind. They are, as we said, 'above the fence'. No man knows anything about them. The future of mankind is a metaphysical question, and only a metaphysical answer can be given to it. Man can only consider the future from its deontological aspect to find out what he must do today, what his present duty is; for the rest, only Faith, confessed or not, can give the answer. If someone has an answer other than that of faith let them give it. Such an answer I, at least, do not know.

Faith, then, tells me that human affairs, have reached a point where God's intervention is inevitable. God *will* intervene. This is what Faith says. Through Faith I can see the coming of the new age. And for all what I said before, I can almost hear the words of the Lord resound in my ears: 'Look round on the fields; they are already white, ripe for harvest.' (John 4, 35) I wait for the Saviour to come and save mankind anew and lead them out of the wood. How He will come I do not know, but it is high time to recall the expectation of the early Church and say with them: 'Amen, come Lord Jesus.'

It is with this expectation and the consciousness of a believer's mission to do his duty today and hope for a better tomorrow, that this book has been written. To the writer it would be a great satisfaction, the greatest satisfaction that any mortal can feel, if his readers—no matter how many or how few, no matter how much they agree or disagree—would at least admit this: The man who wrote these pages has spoken 'from the overflowing of his heart' and said all what a free, unprejudiced vision of life has taught him to say, guided only by truth as he, at least, has seen it!